Peter Ustinov
MY RUSSIA

Macmillan London

First published 1983 by
MACMILLAN LONDON LIMITED
London and Basingstoke
Associated companies in Auckland, Dallas, Delhi, Dublin,
Hong Kong, Johannesburg, Lagos, Manzini, Melbourne,
Nairobi, New York, Singapore, Tokyo, Washington and Zaria

This book was designed and produced by
George Rainbird Ltd
40 Park Street, London W1Y 4DE

ISBN: 0 333 34129 5

Designer: Martin Bristow
Picture researcher: Tom Graves
Indexer: Vicki Robinson

Text filmset by SX Composing Ltd
Rayleigh, Essex, England
Illustrations originated by Adroit Photo Litho Ltd
Birmingham, England
Printed and bound by Brepols s.a.
Turnhout, Belgium

FRONTISPIECE: By the fountains of Peterhof at Leningrad

Contents

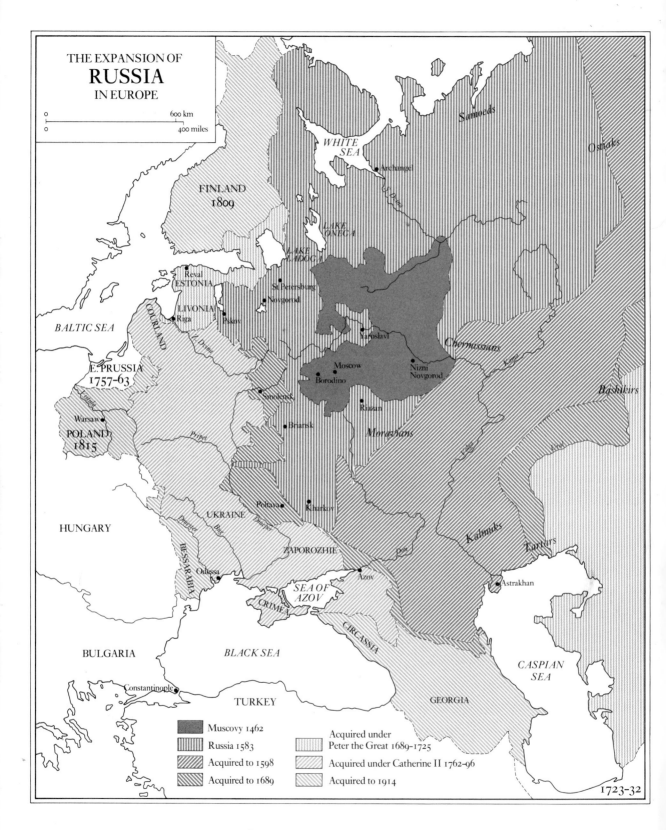

THE EXPANSION OF
RUSSIA
IN EUROPE

0 ——————— 600 km
0 ——————— 400 miles

Samoeds

WHITE
SEA

Archangel

Ostiaks

FINLAND
1809

LAKE
ONEGA

LAKE
LADOGA

Reval
ESTONIA

St Petersburg
Novgorod

BALTIC SEA

LIVONIA
Riga

Pskov

Yaroslavl

Cheremssans

E. PRUSSIA
1757–63

Moscow

Nizni
Novgorod

Kama

Borodino

Bashkirs

Warsaw

Smolensk

Riazan

POLAND?
1815

Pripet

Briansk

Moravians

Volga

HUNGARY

Poltava

Kharkov

Dniester

UKRAINE

Bug

Dnieper

ZAPOROZHIE

Don

Kalmuks

Tartars

BESSARABIA

Odessa

Azov

SEA OF
AZOV

Astrakhan

CRIMEA

CIRCASSIA

BULGARIA

BLACK SEA

CASPIAN
SEA

Constantinople

TURKEY

GEORGIA

▓ Muscovy 1462		Acquired under
Russia 1583		Peter the Great 1689–1725
Acquired to 1598		Acquired under Catherine II 1762–96
Acquired to 1689		Acquired to 1914

1723–32

CHAPTER ONE

Why 'My' Russia?

My Russia. The title is the publishers. At first I feared it might have a pretentious ring, and yet, on second thoughts, it occurred to me that every man has his Russia, his Britain, his America, even, if he knows where it is, his Swaziland, or at least, his mental image of Swaziland. Images can neither be entirely true nor entirely false, since both truth and falsehood are relative, without so much as the benefit of a Richter scale.

My Russia is therefore patently not the Russia of Brezhnev, nor that of Solzhenitsyn, nor yet that of Reagan. As an individual at large in a sea of tide and current, buffeted but not as yet shipwrecked on a shoal of sterile ideology, I have a right to a Russia of my own, and therefore the title, for all its brash simplicity, seems to me a good one.

A great many human, and indeed animal reactions, are caused by fear or the creation of fear. Terms like 'the Yellow Peril' and 'the Sleeping Giant' are redolent of an age-old preoccupation with minotaurs and monsters, unseen Gods of volcano and of forest, who occasionally awake from their untroubled slumbers to wreak frightful vengeances on the anthills of humans in their path. The concept of 'the Yellow Peril' did not mean that the charming waiter in the Chinese restaurant down the road could turn ugly at a moment's notice, but it nevertheless entertained a fugitive but nagging thought that there are a million million of his like, and that if anything happened to wipe the welcoming smile off his face, he would not be without allies.

The phobia which China inspired by virtue of its immense population is equalled by that which Russia evokes by its vast size. The United States and Canada, huge countries by any standards, have four time zones. The Soviet Union has eleven, with over one-sixth of the world's surface. It had every right during the centuries of the great somnolence to the title of 'Sleeping Giant'. Today authorities are unanimous in the opinion that it is awake, and has even learned some of the ropes. As usual in such cases, there are those who wish to humour it, in the belief that it is sensitive to human warmth, and that it has a memory. But there are others, more nervous and therefore more belligerent, who call such endeavours appeasement, and think that a show of strength is what will impress the leviathan.

It is practically impossible for anything very large to be charming. A puppy will steal the limelight from even a well-loved dog, while a lion cub is brimful of feline playfulness without any of the dangers. When fully grown lions wish to play, their motives are often mistaken. The same is true of all large things.

Russia's expansion towards its 'natural' frontiers, 1462–1914.

The advance in communications technology, shrinking the world, has only served to enhance the sense of terror Russia inspires, the victim of her own gigantic proportions. The nervousness Russia induces in the rest of the world has always been present, fed in the past by travellers' tales from the great unknown, and it has only increased as we seem to know her better. It is difficult to credit that such a stupendous bulk can be harmless at least in intention, and that at times even King Kong may wish to play.

Even when a Western public applauds gymnastic teams of lissom young ladies on the brink of puberty, who display either excessive joy or disappointment, or else a rocklike stoicism in the face of defeat or victory, according to their several temperaments, it is difficult to escape the impression that these creatures, touched with physical grace, are not the products of some grey factory of athletes, where an unsmiling rigidity is the rule.

It is our habit to regard their ice-hockey players and soccer teams as automatons, instructed like living chess pieces by some grim mastermind with invisible reins. All this is to confuse the shadow of Russia with the often highly emotional people who shelter there. And it is, of course, the media which perpetuate the mediaeval legends and keep the home fires of prejudice burning. The media, and the politicians who, for all their eloquence, tend to have a particular idea of the present, a portentous view of the future, and very little knowledge of history apart from the mistakes of their immediate predecessors, a subject on which they can debate for hours.

Whereas events in Poland cause alarm, there is general outcry against the conference decisions at Yalta in 1945, as though the history of that part of the world began there. It is alleged that Roosevelt's terminal illness was at the base of all the trouble. There were even those, at the end of the Second World War, who were surprised and disgusted that scant notice was taken of the Polish government in exile in London, who they felt should have been allowed to continue where they had been forced to leave off by Hitler.

Had the French communists of the Resistance formed a government in Paris a few days before the arrival of the Allied troops, would such an arrangement have been tolerated by the Allies? Of course not. Then, Yalta or no Yalta, how can one have expected democratic prerogatives only a decade old to hold sway on the Vistula after the greatest conflict ever known?

Russia is, and always has been, acutely conscious of her security, and for the very best of reasons, bitter experience. She has lost far more men and material on her own soil than on anyone else's!

It is fashionable today to conduct a moderate witchhunt for that pro-Soviet bunch of Cambridge undergraduates and their fellow-travellers who spied for Russia a quarter of a century and more ago. Very few of the interrogators, and certainly none who have appeared on television in this connection, are of an age to remember the atmosphere of that epoch,

A German anti-Bolshevik poster, 1918. The image of terror, but 'at times even King Kong may wish to play'.

BOLSCHEWISMUS
BRINGT KRIEG
ARBEITSLOSIGKEIT UND HUNGERSNOT
KVNSTANSTALT O.CONSÉE
MVNCHEN
VEREINIGUNG ZUR
BEKÄMPFUNG DES BOLSCHEWISMUS
BERLIN W.9 SCHELLINGSTR.2

ГРУДЬЮ НА ЗАЩИТУ ПЕТРОГРАДА!

'Stand firm for Petrograd'

the start of our present chapter of history. It was a time of unspeakable frustration. The Spanish Civil War was raging, and being slowly but inexorably lost by the legitimate government. France, Britain, and the United States were officially neutral, only intellectuals and romantic spirits from those countries throwing themselves into the unequal conflict. Italy and Germany were testing their new weapons and techniques among the ranks of the insurgents. Russia, far away, was helping the government with the relatively slender means at her disposal, while preaching the collective security which was to gain later popularity with such organizations as NATO and the Warsaw Pact, but which, at the time, fell on the deafest of ears.

The dogged inability of Mr Chamberlain and his government to understand that war with Hitler was inevitable led many to believe that the Soviet Union was the last bastion of hope before the merchants of militant nostalgia who were preparing to visit us with the second coming of the Roman Empire and the obscenities of the super race. It was only when the Russians understood that collective security was impossible with those who had a sneaking admiration for the technical powers of fascism, freeways constructed by singing men as naked in mind as in

'Have you volunteered?'

body and railways which ran on time, that they reached the fateful accommodation with Nazi Germany, and provoked cries of moral outrage in the West. What was regarded as the acme of cynicism on the part of the Russians, was also seen as a triumph of opportunism by Hitler, and once again it was the gallant Poles who suffered partition and the prospects of annihilation as a nation.

Naturally the Russian action was not inspired by anything as cumbersome as a moral issue; they were fed up with the negligence and vacillation of the British and French, and their historic sense of what was required for the security of their frontiers dominated their thinking, as it

A rich peasant and a bourgeois, traditional enemies of the Revolution: 'Manifesto: All power to the landowners and capitalists ! ! ! For the workers and peasants – the whip ! ! !'

had when they, the Russians and the Austrians had divided Poland in three some two hundred years before.

Had they allowed the Germans to move right up to their borders, and had the subsequent German advance some two years later been conducted with the same efficiency as it had been in Poland, both Moscow and Leningrad would have surely fallen, while the ability to preserve vital industries and conduct a counter-offensive would have been much reduced. This consideration in the human mind is enough to justify the pact with Hitler.

Once the German offensive had begun, the moral posture of the Allies was conveniently shelved in the archives, and Russia became an heroic partner. It was apparently while Russia was an ally that the notorious

British spies were at their most active, even if they are now being judged by the standards of a cold war. It might be claimed that the sharing of secrets with foreign powers, even allies, is a criminal breach of security, but then the question arises, does this rule apply to the sharing of secrets with the United States, which must have occurred unofficially as well as officially on numerous occasions?

It is difficult for me to understand how anybody can become a spy, even for a financial consideration. I wouldn't know a secret if one came my way, and I certainly wouldn't know how to begin marketing it, so that my sympathy for the victims of such retrospective judgments is qualified. However, their emotional attachments, in view of the crippling ineffectiveness of British policies in the late-nineteen thirties, and the British Government's blindness when faced with the obvious menace of fascism, are crystal clear.

The evident satisfaction with which these tiny scraps of dirt are being unearthed from a past which is beginning to dim is symptomatic both of people's pleasure in evoking a time when Britain still had a glut of secrets worth betraying, and of that constant suspicion of Russia which retains its freshness at all times in the refrigerator of Western consciousness.

An American statesman has claimed that the Soviet Union is the last Imperialist predator, preying on smaller nations. This is merely to say that, in some respects, the Soviet Union is old-fashioned. Predators come in all shapes and sizes these days, often with smiles of benevolence, and Imperialism is not merely the stuff of the military. It has appeared in clerical garb, roasting heretics for the general good, or in the shape of businessmen, opening up markets with strings attached, or yet again in the shape of television, indoctrinating by means of light entertainment. If by Imperialism we mean enslavement, not merely physical, but mental and economic, then it is very far from dead anywhere, and to recognize it in only one shape is merely to engage in propaganda.

Historically, Russia was never an Imperialist power in the conventional sense of the word, in that it was not her habit to venture abroad with the idea of conquest. Her ships did not roam the seas as privateers, nor did she bring the painful benefits of true faith to people who had evolved in peace with other gods. On the rare occasions when the Russians did try such expansionism, they began to feel uncomfortable, as though out of their element, and retired. Admittedly they ventured across the Bering Straits, led by a Danish navigator of that name, and settled in Alaska, mainly as trappers and fur dealers. They received practically no help from St Petersburg, and eventually sold the place to the Americans, a negotiation which was named 'Seward's Folly' at the time. Seward has not had the recognition he deserves since.

The Russians probed far into California at one time, and even occupied one of the Hawaiian Islands for a considerable period, before expressing the belief that it lay within the American zone of influence, and creeping away gratefully to more familiar climes, far from pine-apples and outriggers.

The Russian method of aggrandizement has always been rather different from that of more traditional colonial nations. Since Russians suffer easily from homesickness – in a country so vast it is possible to feel homesick even within its borders – they tend to lean on neighbours' walls until these collapse under their weight, and then help to rebuild them a little further away from where they had been before. Certainly there were battles of conquest, but a great deal was done by erosion, most especially in Asia.

The inherent enmity of the Chinese was certainly kindled by the almost imperceptible advance of Tsarist Russia into the heartlands of Central Asia, while the skirmishes east of the Caspian were legion, and brought them face to face with British interests. Relations with Turkey were perpetually quarrelsome. And so it was that, unlike the Western Empires, theirs grew in one piece, uncluttered with appendages.

This is no place to analyse the morality of empires in general. Suffice it to say that what is today a dirty word, was, a mere half century ago, a clarion-call of enobling righteousness. A pious paternalism was the out-ward expression of those who exploited the weakness of defenceless people with stern efficiency, insensitive to local tradition and self-respect. That they also brought material advantages in the European sense of the word is undeniable, but on the whole the colonial adventure went unappreciated by its victims. Today, of course, everything has been done to eradicate the traces of the colonial presence, or rather to replace that presence with another, the skyscrapers of large commercial interests, eager to help the Third World help itself. Unfortunately in doing so they create privileged classes within these new countries, leaving the underprivileged where they have been more or less for ever.

To oversimplify the problems of the Third World does no service to the truth, and therefore to our comprehension of it. The fact that emerging nations imitate much of the foolish symbolism of imperialism: military rituals, awful national anthems and the like, is an endlessly paradoxical aspect of how the new freedoms are used, and not without its painful absurdity.

The Russian Empire was organized in a different manner, and the possibility existed of integrating the confused territories into the overall administrative structure of the northern country. At the same time, the Russians have always been scrupulous in humouring the national aspira-tions of tribes and peoples, having no inclination towards the concept of the 'melting pot'. It is that romantic notion which has furnished the mystique of Americanism with a starred and striped phoenix rising pure and strong by the dawn's early light from the embers of old world intolerance and stupidity. *E Pluribus Unum*. The Russians, on the contrary, jealously preserved national identity, and even nuances of national identity throughout their Empire and the tradition lives to this day in the many republics and autonomous territories of the USSR.

For a time, during the last century, the Tsar's personal bodyguard, those ultimately responsible for his safety, were composed entirely of potentially troublesome tribal warriors from every one of the peoples making up the Caucasus. And in recent history, many of the nation's leaders have come from the minorities, including Stalin, Beria, and Mikoyan. In a sense, Russia is still an empire, in that she gave up nothing that she had taken, at a time when it was fashionable to do so. The United States never took much, except the Philippines, Puerto Rico and Hawaii. She gave up the Philippines, but as to the others, she is still there. Hawaii has even been accorded statehood.

As for being the last of the predators, this once again is doubtful, since there is unfortunately a type of behaviour which characterizes all powerful or ambitious countries, whatever their politics or practical application of human rights. The rulers of what is glibly called the 'free-world' point to the Soviet tanks in Budapest and in Prague, and the invasion of Afghanistan, to say nothing of the activities of Cubans in Angola and the Horn of Africa and Central America, as proof of Russia's aggressive intention to break free of encirclement and preach its own gospel in parts of the world classically denied to it. Naturally the Russians, stung by the holier-than-thou nature of such accusations, point back at the tragedy of Viet-Nam and Kampuchea, at the Dominican Republic, and at the United States' unswerving if avuncular devotion to the cantankerous and mischievous policies of Israel, in which the voice of a great people is suddenly shrill and unmusical. It can also point at Western countries' close relations with shabby dictators and corrupt governments in their hemisphere, apparently as part of a grandiose doctrine formulated by President Monroe, which is generally treated as an unwritten law by those who adhere to it and as a projection of regional arrogance by those who do not.

What has certainly occurred in our century is that the public sense of morality has become more acute with the awful potential of nuclear power and the consciousness of pollution in a generally overcrowded world. This has inevitably created hostility towards those politicians who attempt to continue the time-honoured hypocrisy which permits selfish policies to be propounded in expressions of high-mindedness. There is a salutary scepticism in the air, and it is perhaps just the right time to examine the history of prejudice to which a nation has been the victim from early in her history to the present day.

A Giant's Childhood

There lies in the Hermitage, that enormous all-embracing museum in Leningrad, an exhibit which has nothing to do with painting, furniture, or jewelry. It is, quite simply, a man with the texture of one of those mangled bits of tyre trucks discard on motorways. Light as balsa-wood, the body lies in one of those frigid containers used to display cheese in supermarkets. It is naked apart from a hessian loin-cloth, but the hair and eyelashes and nails on fingers and toes are still intact, and several teeth still rise from blackened gums. The colour of the hair is red, turning to white in places, and the distance from ankle-bone to the top of his head suggests that he would have stood just about six-foot tall without shoes.

He was found buried in the permafrost of the Arctic Circle together with his horse's head and a chariot. The chariot is so high that the hubs of its wheels are level with the eye of the onlooker, and on top there is a platform with a fringed canopy. He is a warrior, a chief, and he lived over two thousand years ago.

On historical atlases, Russia is empty at that period. Only later do arrows appear in vague, approximative sweeps with the words 'Slavs' or 'Varangians' jutting in the space reserved for the future nation from west or north. This permafrost is a treasure house of relics, preserved like frozen meat below the cold northern soil. The other day a baby mammoth came to light, undigested food still in its stomach. There is something strangely wholesome about this extraordinarily uncomplicated and hermetic means of preservation compared to the battle against time developed by the Ancient Egyptians within the dusty rags of those remarkable mummies.

Who were these nebulous creatures inhabiting the glacial wastes long before the historical atlases bothered with them? Why did they ride in lofty, disproportionate chariots? Were these conning-towers, dominating the flat landscape, or did the wheels with a diameter of some ten feet deal with the snow more easily? It is hard to tell, and yet their artefacts suggest that these people deserve to be discovered. The design of their cloth and trappings around the horse's head seem like peasant designs from a much later age.

The appearance of the man is undoubtedly Nordic. His ginger hair gives him a look quite unlike that of the mummies of the Nile, even though the erosion of the years has bestowed on him that cavernous aquilinity common to those who retain tangible vestiges of life centuries after death. Whatever the truth, the ice must hold countless undiscovered secrets which will emerge when finances make such archaeological operations more generally feasible.

A Persian manuscript showing Tamerlaine besieging Herat. Tamerlaine never reached Moscow and the Mongols eventually forced him out of Russia.

Hitler's hankering after racial purity led him to experiments of unsurpassed obscenity, but as a theory it was basically idiotic, since all purity had been lost irretrievably in the cauldron of history many eons ago. The very acme of purity is, by definition, an alloy. Great wines are the result of judicious blending and of accidents. So are great men, and fools.

This gnarled rubber man in his frozen sleep gives no indication of character, although his voice seems tantalizingly only just out of earshot, and his eyelids could open at any moment.

In the great hithering and thithering of prehistory, tribes seem to have wandered over available landscapes much like holidaymakers searching for space on a crowded beach. When they found it they defended it with the tenacity of animals, and eventually the spot of ground on which they had settled quite arbitrarily became sacred in the speeches of patriots, as though a deity had reserved it for their use before their arrival.

It was the Russians' luck that they settled in places with a great empty unknown stretching to their east, and it was their misfortune for a time that out of this bleak horizon galloped the grinning horsemen of the Golden Horde to retard the development of the Russian nation with their cruelty and greed, but also to enrich that nation with an admixture of another culture. The Mongol invasion was, in a very real sense, the anvil on which the character of the emerging nation was forged, and the dogged patience which has been the hallmark of Russian diplomacy throughout the centuries was learned in subservience to the soft-spoken Khans. When Khrushchev, at a much later date, said, 'We will bury you,' he did not intend to do more than recall that particular ambition of outlasting the opponent which is part of the sleepless vigilance others interpret as suspicion. Naturally the conditioned reflexes of propaganda immediately interpreted this jocular challenge as something sinister and bellicose, and the misapprehension has served the enemies of harmony most faithfully.

But who were these Russians, on the outposts of European culture for some, the outposts of Oriental culture for others? The reputation of 'the Sleeping Giant' has been perpetuated by those fearful of his sheer size and conscious of a vast, untapped potential.

But what of the childhood of the Giant, what of the babyhood?

Did others already suspect how huge he would one day be? Was there a time before the complexes developed? Was he playful before he discovered his strength? It was, in any case, a turbulent and unhappy youth. The Russians, widely dispersed, were under continual pressure from a variety of peoples more bellicose than themselves but with less of an aptitude for survival.

Scythians, Goths, Huns, Khazars, and Sarmatians surrounded them, and often exacted tribute from them, and since they possessed no clear

A portrait of Ivan IV (1530–84) who became known as 'the Terrible'.

The Solokha comb (12.3 x 10cm) made in gold by Greek craftsmen for a Scythian chief in the fifth-fourth century BC.

identity or sense of cohesion, this was a relatively easy and profitable sport. According to Herodotus, agriculture was practised in Russia as long ago as 2000 BC. In those days it was a grain exporting nation and Russian grain went as far as Greece. Apart from growing wheat, barley, oats and hemp they hunted and they fished, and wove coarse cloth. Certainly when we marvel at the extraordinary beauty and sophistication of Scythian gold ornaments, it is understandable that the Russians should have seemed yokels to some of their tormentors. It is also understandable that they became conscious of the mysteries of a more elevated culture through the influence of the Greeks and the Iranians.

At first it was a nation divided into autonomous principalities, not always on good terms with each other, and they fell like ninepins under the domination of the Varangians, a Viking people from the north, and suppliers of the first Tsar, Rurik (862–879), who ruled a mixed community, including the Khazar nation in the south. The capital of the Russian state was Kiev, today the capital of the Ukraine.

But already the envious eyes of marauders had settled on the young state, and the first real invasion of Russian soil occurred in 971 during the reign of Sviatoslav, the fourth Tsar, who was killed in battle by the uncouth Pechenegs. They were followed soon after by the even more sinister Polovtsians, who succeeded in cutting Russia off from the Black Sea, overrunning the Hellenic colonies which had had such an influence on the stripling nation.

It is indicative of the first stirrings of a national consciousness that the first really Russian arts began to flourish at this time and under this external pressure. The earliest epic poets and troubadours began to sing of nationhood and a collective identity, and the techniques of architecture in stone were quickly acquired. The great Tsar Vladimir (980–1015) built the first system of fortifications to protect his country from the nomads of the endless steppes, and, with a prescience that mumbo-jumbo and kowtowing to pagan gods was no longer quite the thing for a developing nation, adopted Christianity in a typically pragmatic manner, reflecting all the nascent prejudices and phobias of his people, and perhaps even their humour.

The legend goes that he did the equivalent of inviting tenders for religious conversion, and received, as was to be expected, immediate replies. Mullahs arrived in their scores, eager to enlist another candidate for Islam. There was a very real possibility of Russia becoming a Muslim nation, the only snag being the rules of abstinence, which made the final submission impossible, since the Russian winter could not be faced without vodka. The mullahs were replaced by rabbis, who crossed the border from every conceivable direction. This was not lost on Vladimir, who told them that there seemed to be something about Judaism which tended to disperse its adherents, while the future of the Russian state would be its unshakeable solidarity.

A modern Russian interpretation of the exploits of Prince Igor, leader of the Polovtsians.

A cardinal arrived, seated in a palanquin, carried by four weary domestics. He brought an invitation for Vladimir to visit Rome. Vladimir looked at him slyly, and told him if he was really as great and powerful as his mode of transport suggested, he should have made an ultimate effort, and travelled on a cloud. As for the invitation, Vladimir half closed his eyes, and murmured, 'No. Bring Rome here.'

Only the Greeks had made no effort to convert the Russians to Orthodoxy. Presumably their geographical proximity made them wonder if this effort would be worth while. The Russians changed their mind for them by destroying a Greek settlement, and mentioning casually that the same would happen to other villages if the Greeks did not send popes *at once* to convert them to the true faith of their choice.

The popes gathered up their robes, and rushed north to prevent any new catastrophes, baptizing whole streets at a time. The only awkwardness encountered during this extraordinary affair was in finding a suitable substitute for Perium, the pagan God of Fire, much feared and respected in a land of huge forests, and by a people which had emerged from forests to occupy the plains. A solution was found when the shrines to this frightening and capricious figure were given over to Elijah, who seemed to fit the role by virtue of his ascension in a fiery chariot.

One characteristic was already emerging from all this, and that was the capacity of the Russians to absorb those who initially sought to dominate them. The Varangians are believed to have entered history at the invitation of the republic of Novgorod, which tried to put an end to the quarrels of local princes by offering leadership to a foreigner. called Hzözekz whose name was Russianized as Rurik. The next ruler, Oleg, was called Helgi. The third, Igor or Ingvar, gravitated south towards the great system of rivers which constituted the trade route to Byzantium. The commercial treaty signed between Igor and Byzantium in AD 945 contains, on the Russian side, fifty Norse names and only three Slavonic ones. And yet Igor's son, Sviatoslav, already had a Russian name, as did all subsequent Tsars. Those who came to lead, and to conquer, gradually were absorbed into a way of existence foreign to them. The same was true of religion. Even though the Bible had already been translated into the archaic Slavonic tongue in the course of the ninth century, and the Russian Orthodox Church was, of its own volition, dependent on the Patriarchate of Constantinople for a couple of centuries, the Russians eventually broke free of this dependence and the Church adopted a more national and local character.

It is often assumed that Russia entered history rather later than other European countries, and that she was in her way as isolated as Japan, lost in immense distances, in thraldom to ignorance. The opposite is true. Tsar Yaroslav gave asylum to two of the sons of Edmund, fleeing the wrath of King Canute. He also looked after the banished Harald Hardrada. A daughter of his married Henri I of France.

The relations between states and voyagers existed long before history began to record them. The effigies on the walls of Aztec monuments, notably the Hall of the Ambassadors at Chichen Itza, in Yucatan, show us strange visitors who appear to be wearing kilts. Although Christopher Columbus is credited with the so-called discovery of America, there must be at least a suspicion that he was, in fact, no more than the first tourist. To judge by the millions who have followed in his footsteps, this in no way detracts from his importance.

Be that as it may, the discovery of Arabian and Anglo-Saxon coins and artefacts dating back to the ninth century along those gigantic Russian waterways proves that commerce flourished far away from the better-known avenues very long ago.

Kiev, in the first flush of its importance acquired a cathedral of some magnificence, churches and monasteries. Also the earliest document of Russian law was revised under the name of *Russkaya Pravda* (Russian truth, or law). Everything seemed set for a rapid flowering into a golden age, with the development of a national style, engineering skills, and laws of alarming subtlety and complication. And yet, its primordial trading importance was already threatened by the presence of the terrifying Polovtsians, who cut its access to the Black Sea. More and

The battle between the people of Novgorod and the Suzdal', one of their dependencies, c. 1460.

more Russians looked northwards for safety, and the city of Moscow began to acquire importance after the humblest of beginnings.

Novgorod had always been a city of great individuality, lying to the northwest of Moscow, a kind of Hansa Staat trading with the West and the Scandinavian north. As Kiev declined, Novgorod alone of all Russian towns, became a republic. It was ruled by a popular assembly which elected its civic officers and looked to outside potentates only for its defence. Its trading capacity was enormous, and its dominion extended to the Ural mountains and to the far north. Contacts with the rest of Europe were constant, and it was perhaps the most Western expression of Russianness in the whole of history until Peter the Great made conscious efforts to open windows and break down doors with the creation of St Petersburg, or Leningrad, to this day called by derisive Muscovites 'the greatest museum in Russia'. Leningraders call Moscow 'the greatest village in Russia'. Both allegations have elements of truth in them. But Novgorod in its heyday was something quite unique.

When Vladimir adopted Orthodoxy he aroused the immediate hostility of all the rest of Europe, on purely religious grounds.

After the invasions of the nomads, there followed a crusade of Swedes, and no sooner was that over than the Teutonic knights from Livonia set out on crusade, motivated by the most elevated of religious motives, a

The walls of Novgorod

24

refusal to tolerate heresy. The fifth and by far the most terrible invasion, however, came once again from the east. In the six years between 1237 and 1242 the Tartars attempted a mass extermination of Russians. There were only two hundred households left in the great city of Kiev. All the treasures accumulated over three hundred years of cultural growth were utterly destroyed. Those who survived the horror were led away into captivity. For a century and a half the progress initiated by the Varangian grand dukes was halted. Crushing taxes were imposed by the conquerors and they indulged in periodic orgies of slaughter, tempering their murderous outbursts with a curious tact, as when they placed the Orthodox Church under the protection of the Khan. The Tartar power was centered on the Volga, and swept on to new conquests in Poland, Hungary, Romania, Bulgaria, and even Germany and Austria, but they quickly withdrew to deal exclusively with Russia.

Although Novgorod and Moscow held out, together with a few minor principalities, other parts of the country had a more difficult and contentious time of it. In 1336, Galicia managed to free itself of the Tartar yoke, and was immediately gobbled up by the Catholic kingdom of Poland.

The grand duchy of Lithuania, from its capital of Vilna, then called Novagordska, gradually eroded away other Russian areas, such as Polotsk, and eventually Kiev itself. Ironically Russian became the official State and Court language of the Lithuanian crown. By the beginning of the fourteenth century, Lithuania extended from the Baltic to the Black Sea. Even Moscow itself only narrowly escaped incorporation within this massive state, and it seemed for a moment as if the whole of the little that was left of Russia would lose its identity irrevocably. In 1569 the decline of Lithuania resulted in it being absorbed into the powerful kingdom of Poland. This meant that Moscow and the north, exhausted by the endless humiliations of the Tartar occupation and the dark age which followed, was isolated from that other Russia of the south, known as Little Russia, or the Ukraine, which fell under the Polish crown, and whose language became impregnated with Polish words. And this until the middle of the seventeenth century.

Does this seem a likely childhood and adolescence for a giant? Well, it may go some way to explain the big fellow's character.

Ivan the Terrible

In a very real sense, Russia protected Europe from the Mongol invasions by absorbing the brunt of the assault. Perhaps this has been her historic destiny. In the First World War, it would be unreasonable to claim that she had done more than contribute to the ultimate victory of her allies, but a good argument can be advanced for the claim that she saved the war from being lost, by virtue of her prompt mobilization, and rapid engagement of the large armies of the Central Powers for the first three years of hostility. Once again, in the Second World War, with twenty million dead, her part in the final victory cannot be doubted but her role was to take the full weight of the Nazi *blitzkrieg*, and to turn it into a war of attrition, wasteful of both energy and material.

The Tartars careered about Eastern Europe like a storm at sea, only to retire to the vastness of the broad Volga, and make a meal of Russia, and the pickings fallen by the wayside. Their methods were subtle and devious, and at their feet, the Russians were able to observe them at work, and draw their own conclusions. In warfare, each new technique inspires an antidote, and the Russians, defenceless before these men of genteel ferocity, learned both how to swallow their pride and bide their time.

Moscow, relatively far away from the terror of the Golden Horde, began to gain in importance as the centre of gravity shifted from the sunkissed south to the grimmer yet safer north. Since pressure from outside invariably encourages unity, Moscow gradually assumed the importance of a focal point of the Russian resistance.

It is safe to say, however, that for the Russians the greatest historical enemy in time of peace and friend in time of war has been distance, and even in those early days it began to give a very different colour and character to the various parts of the lands settled by the Russian tribes. Far from the urban centres with their Kremlins, and their particular social structures, varying from the sophistication of Novgorod to the tighter hierarchies of Moscow, Tver and their principalities, each with councils, kinds of premature Soviets, there stretched sparsely populated territories under the nominal rule of absent dukes, where illiterate peasants, far from the influence of Europe, laboured like slaves, prey to the caprices of often corrupt and fickle overseers.

All the Russian princes paid tribute to the Tartar Khans, and depended upon them for their power and influence over their own people. During this long night of degradation, the princes even involved the Khans in their own internecine quarrels, and like quislings toadying to Hitler at a later date, they frequently travelled to Sarai, the Tartar capital on the Caspian, in order to seek help against their nearest

Russian rivals, and to receive haughty and shameful treatment for their pains. While the Tartars dealt with a divided house, elements of which came for aid to deal with other elements, it was too easy for the interlopers, and yet beneath the humiliation a finer fibre was taking shape. The dice was loaded in these games of chance, always in the Tartars' favour, but the longer the Russians came to lose their earnings in this vicious casino, the more they began to understand the rules which prevailed there. It was to the credit of the Dukes of Moscow that they mastered these rules more ably, and more quickly than their rivals.

Dmitri Donskoi in Archangel Cathedral, visiting the tomb of his ancestors before going to fight Mamai Khan.

Slowly at first, with the blessings of the Khans, Moscow began to extend its dominion. The upper reaches of the Volga fell, then other important principalities, until the leaders of the Orthodox Church decided to settle in Moscow, when the grandiloquent title of Grand Duke of All the Russias was used for the first time in history.

The Russians felt strong enough with the rapid centralization of power, and a growing sense of national identity, to make their bid for total independence from the Tartars in 1380. Under the leadership of the Grand Duke Dmitri Donskoi, the Russians inflicted a crushing defeat on the Golden Horde, under the leadership of Mamai Khan, on the field of Kulikovo. It was the first real victory of Russian arms if you except the battle won by Alexander Nevsky against the Teutonic

Ivan III overcame the 'mighty Lord Novgorod' and ended Russian subservience to the Mongols in 1480.

knights on the frozen Lake Peipus in 1260. That was a local engagement when compared to the immense and savage battle waged against the greater enemy, during which the casualties on both sides were enormous.

Despite this remarkable feat of arms, Moscow was occupied by the Tartar only two years later, and burned to the ground. However, rifts were beginning to appear in the fabric of the Golden Horde as decadence set in, and Tokhtamish, the conqueror of Moscow, was in his turn routed by Timur, another Khan. From now on, although Moscow continued to pay tribute to the Tartars, the sums were reduced in size, and their delivery dates were not always respected. The growth of Moscow made the enforcement difficult, and in any case, there was a drift of Tartars seeking employment in the big city, much as southern workers from the predominantly agricultural regions come in droves towards the little luxuries of the industrial north today.

Eventually the tributes were merely lip-service to a miserable past, a bad habit it was hard to shake off altogether, a pittance for old-time's sake. After another century, they stopped altogether, not as a result of any peremptory gesture, or a second feat of arms, but because suddenly there was neither supply nor demand. The Russians had eroded the power of the Khans by patience, meeting duplicity with duplicity, ferocity with humility, cruelty with fatalism, and finally learning how to outlast a conqueror by catering to his whims while giving him enough rope to hang himself with in the guise of a gift.

Despite the fact that Moscow lorded it over less than half of the Russian territories, it had become the undoubted figurehead and mind of the nation. Then, at the end of the fifteenth century, the Tartar influence disappeared altogether, with the result that Moscow found nothing in the way of further aggrandizement. The principalities of Tver and Ryazan, which had doggedly opposed Moscow for so long, fell like overripe fruit into her lap. Even proud Novgorod, the so-called 'mighty Lord Novgorod', with its gesture towards democratic government, knuckled under, together with its dependencies, and nothing now stood in the way of recognizable nationhood with a centralized government under an absolute monarch. Gone were the whims of individual princelings, gone were the experiments with autonomous social structures. As Russia felt her muscles, she froze into a stiffly ordered oligarchy, and began to contemplate herself in the mirror of the times.

Under Ivan III, palaces and churches were built, and the Kremlin was extended into an agglomeration which reflected a sense of destiny, even if Italian architects were imported to adjust the style to something less simple than the traditional and very beautiful Russian buildings of the past. At the same time, all was not so quiet on the administrative front.

The aristocracy, which had enjoyed a great deal of local autonomy under the regime of the princes, still entertained considerable ambitions as a class in the new centralized government. These were resisted by the Grand Dukes, and the culmination of these internal struggles came in 1564, when Ivan IV, with his unenviable soubriquet 'the Terrible', introduced the drastic code called the *Oprichnina*, by which the aristocracy was brutally assaulted, its lands confiscated, and handed over to minions of the Crown. Seventeen years earlier, Ivan had had himself elevated to the rank of Tsar of All the Russias in the course of a splendid coronation, and had even claimed, with the help of sycophantic researchers, that the Russian royal family actually descended, not from Rurik and the Varangians from the north, but from the Byzantine and Roman Emperors, more specifically Caesar Augustus, whom all considered a worthy ancestor for a man called 'Terrible'.

Ivan, the penultimate ruler of the Varangian dynasty, was a Dostoevskian character whose odyssey was very similar to some others of the late-Middle Ages, but, at the same time his development and his reactions to those around him was peculiarly Russian and worthy of examination before leaving this dense and incredibly eventful page of history.

At the age of three, when Ivan ascended the grand Ducal throne, he had not yet earned his unenviable name of *Grozny*, which means grim or menacing rather than terrible, although everything was done to that end by the odious gaggle of boyars who left their guilty fingerprints all over the early records of their country. First of all, his mother died, it is believed of poison. In such an entourage it is the most natural of suppositions. Then his nurse was thrown into prison. The boy was left alone with his retarded brother, Giorgi, and a monk, Sylvester. They were neglected, and Ivan later claimed that they had little to eat, and were constantly cold. The kennels were a friendlier playground than the palace, and there the youthful ruler and his brother escaped from surveillance and could relax.

As a rule they were left in rags, more or less to their own devices, but on state occasions they were dressed in magnificent garments and the hideous boyars bowed before in a show of subservience which contained the seeds of almost Biblical mockery, but then the boyars were well versed in religious lore. Considering his Dickensian upbringing, continually showered with paradox, watching the venal aristocrats at work and play, Ivan developed in a remarkably ordinary way, showing no particular predilections or fads. He was, however, doing that very Russian thing, biding his time. His capacity for hatred grew with his suppressed desire for revenge, and even extended to an outsized sense of justice. Suddenly one day he sat on the throne of his own volition, choosing his own robes, and announced the arrest of Andrei Shuisky, the most influential of the boyars. Alarmed by what seemed to him an unforeseeable rabid rage of a household pet, Shuisky fled, but was caught and killed. To their horror, the boyars realized that the neglected

A fully armed soldier from the court of
Ivan IV, 'the Terrible'.

MAGNUS DUX MOSCOVIÆ

cub had come of age, and learned his lesson by just watching them in
silence and without complaint.

It was shortly afterwards that Ivan proclaimed himself the first Tsar
and Caesar in history, and chose a wife from among the Romanovs, who
had always refrained from joining in the intrigues of the boyars, an
abstinence which was to stand them in good stead later on, when Mikhail
was elected after the extinction of the line of Rurik. This wife was very
young and very attractive, and certainly, during her short life gave him
both love and tenderness. He reciprocated by calling her his 'Little
Heifer'. When she died, he sobbed, 'My little heifer has departed'. In
the foetid atmosphere of his palace, where every column could hide a
potential murderer, and where the night was peopled with the shadows
thrown by guttering candles, he believed that his bride had been poisoned, and revenged himself on all and sundry to be sure of having punished
the culprit. He married six times more, but it was never the same.

31

Lonely and suspicious, he extended his personal bodyguard to over five thousand men, a collection of rowdies and drinking partners he dressed from head to foot in black in caustic immitation of monkish habits, and referred to this motley crowd of deserters from foreign armies, renegade boyars and roisterers of unknown origin, as his brothers. This continuous desire to identify with the opposite end of the social scale is another characteristic Russian trait, the burning wish to attain great heights from the bottom, and conversely to lower oneself from the heights to the depths of degradation. It may be that a hope of understanding the very meaning of life lies at the base of this endless process, in which the magnificence of a ceremony is regarded as a vain, glorious conceit moments later, and the vestments of office are discarded as mortal folly. Ivan was prey to these abrupt changes of heart, and was never more himself than when drinking, torturing and killing with his cronies, dressed as them, in black. And he always made a very careful

The first map of Russia by an Englishman, Anthony Jenkinson, made in 1570. 'Foreigners' were already seeing Russia as 'a sleeping giant' – a great unknown peopled by savages.

A procession of boyars followed by merchants carrying furs for trade. From a woodcut print by Michael Peterle, 1576.

note of the identity of his victims, so that he could be privileged to pray for the immortality of their souls at a later date.

Just as Ivan claimed to be the heir of the Roman Emperors and the only true prophet in a sea of heretics and compromisers so too, at a later date, did Hitler. Like Ivan, Hitler found it necessary to buttress his position with all manner of specious racial theories as a justification for his distant, mystic look, and Mussolini believed himself to be the recipient of some Olympic torch from the hands of the ghostly legionnaires of Imperial Rome. The hot air which flows around pragmatic actions of selfish and greedy autocrats always has much the same odour, sickening in its intensity and yet as transitory as time itself.

As for the luxury of having a religion of your very own, it should be remembered how satisfying it was for Henry VIII of England to divorce his way out of the clutches of Catholics, and invent something new and snug, the Church of England. Ivan, too, felt comforted by the fact that state and church could work hand in glove and hand on heart in the interests of a god of their own, bending his ear to Russian problems, which was another way of saying his problems.

And these were many. First of all, although Russia could, by now, be relied on to put up an outward show of magnificence whenever the occasion demanded it, there was really precious little to back up the facade. The Court life was considered uncouth by those with experience of such things, and neither the arts nor crafts were a match for the rich achievements of the West. Ivan desperately wanted Western contacts and Western trade, but he was denied the necessary outlets by a *cordon sanitaire* of hostile nations who mistrusted the potential power of his armies, and did all they could to lock him out of Europe. The Black Sea was, by now, well within the Ottoman Empire, while Sweden straddled the Baltic together with Livonia. It took an English seafarer, Richard Chancellor, to open up the Arctic trading route with the White Sea in the 1550s, but this was only open for a small portion of the year, and Russia could hardly be expected to hang the weight of her commercial hopes on this slender, seasonal thread. Still, it is strangely touching to remember that as a result of this English maritime initiative, a group of grubby Russian boyars eventually landed in England as a delegation with the express purpose of finding a wife for Ivan the Terrible at the court of Queen Elizabeth I. They lodged at Greenwich and it is pleasant to think that it was the only address they brought back with them to Moscow, and consequently the obvious place for Peter the Great to go when his time for lodging came. The eye of these bearded and insalubrious men eventually fell on Lady Mary Hastings as an ideal choice for Ivan, and when that lady-in-waiting heard of the promotion

Ivan's cruelty reached its climax when he fatally injured his son by striking him in a rage with a heavy staff. From a painting by Ilya Repin.

34

The Church of the Transfiguration
in Novgorod

which destiny had reserved for her, she fell into an immediate stupor, a reaction which pained the boyars who imagined themselves to be the bringers of great joy. Queen Elizabeth herself eventually persuaded the delegation that probably Ivan the Terrible would feel happier in the long run with some more homespun virginity, to whom the violence and suspicion of the ageing monarch would come as less of a surprise.

There came a moment for Ivan when individual victims no longer sufficed, and he attacked a city, Novgorod. The river which runs through it was red with blood. And then the climax of his reign was attained, a climax both tragic and absurd. In his dotage, he pinned all his hopes on his son Ivan, the fruit of his beloved 'heifer's' womb, the reminder of happier times. In a fit of unaccountable rage, he struck his son with the heavy metal pommel of his staff of office, and the young man died three days later. At least there was no doubt about the nature of the old Tsar's prayers. He himself died within two years.

CHAPTER FOUR

Troubled Times

In the light of our knowledge of the modern Russian state, some of the reforms introduced in the latter half of the sixteenth century are of the greatest interest. For example, to go ahead and serve foreign interests in any capacity whatever was judged to be treason. Whereas Russia had never known real feudalism in the European sense of the word, serfdom was now generally introduced as a form of military and organizational necessity, a permanent mobilization of the nation, in which the system did not extend merely to the serfs themselves, who were much like private soldiers, but to the other classes of society as well, who were commissioned or non-commissioned officers according to their rank in the hierarchy. The entire structure of state was geared for a permanent emergency, taxes being imposed according to the military obligations of the serf-owners, and incentives being given to landed gentry as a counterweight to the incessant claims and clamour of the ancient aristocracy. As soldiers in an army, peasants were expressly forbidden to leave the estates on which accidents of birth had deposited them, and migrate to other estates.

What engendered this extraordinarily rigorous policy of the tight rein, which has come down to the present day despite all the upheavals and revolution?

It cannot be divorced from the attitude of Russia's neighbours whose instinctive misgivings about the direction the new empire was taking became rapidly contagious. For the first time the Russians' successes against the Swedish and Livonian armies raised concern in Europe, as the presence of a new power in the known world began to be felt. And once again, it is uncanny, with reference to modern times, that the first voices to cry out in alarm against a menace to world peace came jointly from Poland and the Vatican, the former in fear of Russia's military strength, but both to halt the spread of heresy. Not all nations, however, saw the threat as real. The British, for instance, were extending their trade, as were all the nations of the north not engaged in active hostilities with the Russians, and more and more foreign artisans, technicians and craftsmen began to settle in Moscow, seeing there a huge potential market for practically anything manufactured and designed.

Ivan had managed to acquire a tenuous foothold on the Baltic but lost it again, and the tight rein practically choked the nation on the bit. When he died in 1584, his weak son Fyodor took over, and with the subsequent relaxation of authority, the state began slowly to disintegrate. The alarms sounded by the Poles and the Vatican had been premature. Russia was not yet ready to assume her final shape. Her strength had been sapped in the effort of growth, and now the country gradually lost

The interior of the Terem Palace in the Kremlin. Reconstruction of the Kremlin was begun by Ivan III and continued during the reign of Ivan the Terrible. It symbolized Moscow's growing awareness of its civic and religious dignity.

its way. Boris Godunov, a man of some intelligence and vision, remembered today as the hero of a tragic opera rather than as a real person, became regent, with the avowed intention of carrying out the policies of Ivan the Terrible, but found himself opposed by the boyars, who had fewer scruples in contradicting him than they had in standing in Ivan's path. With the death of the feckless Fyodor in 1598, Boris, riddled with self-doubt, proclaimed himself Tsar, which was doubtless a bad decision. Despite the fact that the only real heir to the throne, Dmitri, had been safely assassinated in 1591, the boyars came up with a hastily groomed false Dmitri, having run to the Poles for help much as they had run to the Tartars for favours against their kith and kin in the past.

It must be emphasized that class warfare has been a consistent element throughout Russian history, and that duty to a class often took precedence over duty to a nation. In a sense, this was an almost universal tendency throughout history before the development of formal nationalism, but the Russians seem to have pursued this tendency to its logical conclusion and beyond, which is perhaps an explanation of the violence vented on the bourgeoisie and aristocracy in the early days of the Russian revolution, and the readiness of the populace to identify Marx's division of society into rigid classes.

Be that as it may, in 1605, two months after Godunov's mysterious death, the false Dmitri turned up in Moscow, with the help of the Poles. He did not last long, however. His debauches and the evident Catholicism of his entourage were enough to turn his supporters against him, and they incited a mob to murder him only a few months after his triumphant arrival.

From here on tragedy and drama declined into *Grand Guignol*. So excessive were the demonstrations of cupidity, so charged the outbursts of hatred, and so utterly crazy the ambition, superstition, and absurdity of the principal players, even Shakespeare would have found it impossible to invest the shower of occurrences with either logic or motivation.

After the death of Boris and the killing of the false Dmitri a member of the ancient aristocracy, Vassili Shuisky, became Tsar in 1606. Reasonably enough, under the circumstances, he undertook to stop the indiscriminate slaughter of his own class, which had been a favourite pastime of Ivan the Terrible, but this gesture of understanding towards the richest in the land was not of great use to him, since a new class of rural gentry had become the predominant influence in the growing vacuum. New forces appeared on the scene in the form of renegade serfs and Cossacks, and there were many local rebellions, the most significant being one led by a serf in the south. The parts of the country further from Moscow were in open upheaval, and to stir the muddied waters even more, a second false Dmitri put in an appearance, demanding allegiance, and challenging the role of Tsar Vassili. In case all this seems very Russian, it is perhaps time to remind ourselves that England also

The murder of the false Dmitri in 1606

had its Perkin Warbeck and Lambert Simnel, although admittedly, they staked their claims a littler earlier. Perhaps this is a case of the Russians being a little indiscriminate in their imitation of the West.

Vassili, rendered nervous by the wavering of the boyars, some of whom seemed ready to back the new imposter, went one better than to appeal to the Tartars or the Poles. He appealed to the Swedes which not unnaturally riled the Poles since they liked an exclusivity of treachery. Sigismond, King of Poland, beat Charles IX of Sweden to the punch, and appeared close to Moscow. The boyars promptly deposed Vassili, and left the throne empty for a while, preferring undefinable chaos to a definable Polish presence.

They were fickle as ever, nevertheless, and eventually reached a compromise by offering the Russian throne to young Vladislav, the son of the ambitious Sigismond. As so often happens with compromises, they fail to satisfy all parties to a dispute. Although the boyars voluntarily opened the gates of Moscow to a Polish army, and were willing to submit to Polish overlordship on condition that their rights and habits were respected along with those of the powerful landed gentry, Sigismond did not see why his young son should be honoured in this way, and

A seventeenth-century English map of Tartary

desired this attractive throne for himself. This act of braggadocio was resented by the people, who were prepared for a Polish prince who could be moulded into Russian ways, but had no desire for a Polish king already hardened in Polish ways. Under these conditions, the Second False Dmitri immediately seemed almost authentic to the Russians, and they flocked to his banner, only to be stopped in their tracks when their new idol was butchered by, of all things, a Tartar of his bodyguard. Now it was time for the clergy to enter the fray against the Catholics in the Kremlin, and they incited the leaders of the landed gentry and a Cossack army to take matters into their own hands, and the Poles found themselves in the uncomfortable position of being locked into the sinister fastness, and surrounded on all sides. But once again dissension broke out in an almost ludicrous fashion among those investing the Kremlin. As the result of an argument, presumably about strategy, the Cossacks killed the leader of the landed gentry and they withdrew from the siege in disgust, only to reform an army elsewhere which was pledged to protect what was left of the country until such a time as a representative leader could be found. This new army was specifically required to refuse all assistance from the Cossacks, not only for the very good reason that they had had more help from the Cossacks than they really needed, but because those wild men were spreading like a plague all over the northern parts of Russia, living on the land, raping and robbing, an activity in which they were joined by rampaging Poles.

The new army began as the stuff of which legends are made. It was led by two men of widely differing characters and background, Dmitri Pozharsky, a prince, and Kuzna Minin, a butcher. Behind them stood the authority of the Church in the person of the patriarch Germogen. As it marched towards Moscow its ranks were swelled by peasants and serfs, hungry and tired of the terrible uncertainties of their existence. It was as though the threat to survival had created a mystic sense of unity, much as that which spurred them to superhuman efforts later against both Napoleon and Hitler. The army arrived before Moscow in July 1612, and found the Cossacks already investing the capital into which King Sigismond had rushed Polish reinforcements. The Cossacks regarded the arrival of a prince, a butcher, and a rabble as an intrusion into their own solution to the problem. These Cossacks were frontiersmen, whose identity was established during the wars against the Tartars. They began as posses, and eventually became rough and ready adventurers, sometimes employed as mercenaries, but they were more addicted to their liberty of action and their crude sense of justice, much in the manner of the pioneers of the American West. Just as the latter opened up the West, the Cossacks were destined to open up the Russian East, moving into empty territories like men staking claims on unoccupied land and searching for sources of natural wealth.

At this time, however, their ambition was to impose their will on the Poles in the Kremlin, and then, presumably, to influence the future of the nation by their free, easy, and ferocious country ways. Once again, they quarrelled with their allies, and left Minin and Pozharsky to conduct the battle alone, retiring to sulk in the background. At the height of the action, however, they were infected by that sudden sense of Russianness which became contagious as the focus narrowed and sharpened to show the situation in all its terrible simplicity. With wild cries, the Cossacks joined in the battle on the side of the peasant army, and the Poles surrendered.

In 1613, a *zemsky sobor*, or Popular Parliament met in Moscow to elect a new Tsar. In the contemporary mind, the image conjured up by Russia is one of endless autocracy, but the very opposite is the truth, at least intermittently. The Russians have always placed great reliance on discussion, council and a vote. After all, the very word 'Soviet' means council, or committee. And now, in 1613, every grade of society was represented in this great popular manifestation, and the winner of the election was a young man of only seventeen, the son of a priest who was a nephew of Ivan the Terrible's first wife. He had the advantage of not being a member of the ancient aristocracy, and he could therefore not be

The entry of Mikhail Romanov into Moscow on 2 May 1613.

used as a tool by the boyars, and yet he was well enough placed in the hierarchy to command respect. And Mikhail Romanov was Russian. The *zemsky sobor* remained in session for three years in order to help the young Tsar in his perilous job, and to show the solidarity which the nation so badly needed. The collaboration of all classes with the Tsar worked so promisingly, despite the return from Polish captivity of the Tsar's father, the powerful patriarch Filaret, that the work of this national council was extended for a further term of three years.

The price of peace was the surrender of the Finnish littoral to the Swedes, and the old Russian city of Smolensk became Polish in a readjustment of the frontier. But there was to be no finality about these changes. At the same time as trying to re-establish order, the government completely reorganized the army, inviting soldiers of fortune from overseas to lead it, and even being willing to hire whole battalions of mercenaries. There was a pragmatism evident in its *revanchard* sentiments which was to become typical. If it needed a humiliation to win, then the price was acceptable. It had already worked with the Tartars. The Russians had learned to swallow their pride with their daily bread, showing nothing on their faces but the expressionless image of patience.

To this day, the expression has not altered, especially among the old. There is a stillness about people in the street which suggests a morose indifference to the others around them, and yet beneath this evident detachment there lies a huge potential for emotion and turmoil. It is as though the temperature is instinctively kept at a low level because people know the high levels of passion of which they are capable. Even today, with a bland press and a television which deals not in controversy but in items of general interest in a quiet and carefully modulated way, there is a sentiment not at all of ruthless dictatorship, but of a cossetting of the spirit, an approach to news so reasonable as to steer close to somnolence at times.

Certainly an imposition of American norms of information on the Russians would be a disaster. For instance, the considerable time devoted to the reports of homicides, with hand-held cameras focussing on

Tsar Mikhail, the founder of the Romanov dynasty

corpses casually strewn over fire-escapes and sidewalks stained with blood, and the relaxed reports of policemen and witnesses, would scandalize the Soviet viewer, who would consider that if such squalid phenomena must exist, they should be relegated to the militia, who are trained to deal with them, and not be exhibited on the TV screen, where children could inadvertently have access to them.

It may seem curious to draw attention to such coeval speculations at this juncture of a brief historical survey, but the period of history entitled the 'Time of Troubles' (1604–1613) with exquisite understatement, illuminates aspects of the Russian character still much in evidence today. There is no Latin volatility, no passing showers and emollient sunshine here, no brief outbursts and tearful reconciliation. When the Russian sky begins to glower, the possibilities are as endless as the horizon, and there will be ample time for every single possibility to show itself. Fate has no need to hurry.

Peter the Great was one who liked to mix with the common people to be aware of what was being said and what was being plotted. On his travels he lived extremely simply, leaving the majesty to those who enjoyed such sports. Alexander I vanished incognito into a monastery at a later date, no longer wishing to be identified as a potentate in retirement, and the duality was carried even further by the great soldier, Suvorov, who affected the uniform of a private soldier during battles, and when drunk and obstreperous after his innumerable victories, was brutally called to order by his batman with the previously rehearsed dialogue. 'Bedtime', the orderly would shout. 'By whose orders?' Suvorov cried. 'By the orders of His Excellency Field Marshal Prince Suvorov-Rimnitsky,' yelled the orderly. Suvorov paled, stood stiffly to attention, and murmured, 'He must be obeyed,' and tottered quietly to his bed.

There is a will to extend the frontiers of experience in many people. Sadists, or those who dream of unreasonable power, are often meek little creatures of unexceptional appearance, while those who seek humiliation in the brothels of the world are sometimes captains of industry, cabinet ministers, or bishops, those with endless decisions to make and not so much as a tinge of servility in their daily routine. The French call this strange craving for the depths, *Nostalgie de la Boue*, making the phenomenon much more poetic and human than in the forbidding formula of psychiatry. It certainly exists, and perhaps the Russians are more prey to it than most others. At all events, Russians are capable of immense acts of faith, and equally immense acts of renunciation, as though their pendulum swings higher than other people's and on many occasions more unpredictably.

The extraordinary hysteria which the collapse of the state into the 'Time of Troubles' engendered was remarkable even by prevailing standards. When the first false Dmitri occupied the throne, he took a

Polish wife, Marina. When Dmitri was deposed and killed some eleven months later, Marina succeeded in escaping. Then when the second false Dmitri claimed the throne, Marina emerged from hiding, and greeted him as her husband, although he bore no physical resemblance to the first Dmitri. When the second Dmitri was killed in his turn, Marina eloped with a savage chieftain from the south, but this time, presumably in the interests of a relatively quiet domestic life on horseback, she made no claim that he was a third Dmitri.

And all this was followed by the populace with the urgency which a popular television series inspires in the people today. The only difference being that in those days the action was live, and the corpses were dead.

Peter the Great

Obviously the news which filtered out of these bloody events caused concern abroad, but it is not enough to explain the image of menace which Russia had already begun to acquire. At the outset of Ivan's long reign, when the country was relatively calm by the standards of those days, Queen Elizabeth I's ambassador felt himself able to report to his monarch that every man lived in peace, 'enjoying and knowing his own; good officers placed, justice administered everywhere'. And yet, he sensed the distant flickering of lightning and the growl of thunder beyond the line of trees and the wooden houses. He added to his letter, 'God hath a great plague in store for His people.'

From the outset, it had not been easy for the Russians. The powers of the West had well-defined frontiers, largely because they had access to the sea. Despite troubles with the Scots and Welsh the English borders were, on the whole, evident. France, while still divided internally, was emerging as a cohesive, French-speaking entity, with her northern, western and southern confines clearly marked by the sea or mountain ranges. Spain had troubles with Portugal, but once the Moors were ejected, Spain was contained comfortably within the Iberian peninsula.

No threat had ever developed across the Atlantic, which was, on the contrary, a beckoning ocean with promises of untold wealth.

Sweden too was a nation in a precise shape marked by the Baltic, and it was only in the East that it was for ever adjusting its dominion. Germany and Italy were still agglomerations of small states, and their tardy unions were to cause great havoc later on, when the joys of nationhood were to lead them to colonial adventures after all the best bits had already been taken. Eventually, frustrated by their unfulfilled dreams of power in the undeveloped world, they turned on Europe. But all that was far off at this time. To the East lay the *cordon sanitaire* of Catholic nations, Livonia, ruled by the so-called brothers of the sword, a military and religious order blessed by the Pope, and Poland. And what lay beyond? Not an ocean, full of promise, but *terra incognita* from which terrible apparitions had suddenly materialized, wild horsemen from another world, in search of slaves and tribute, pirates from whose rapid if impermanent displacements there was no escape. And further south, there were the Turks, another more organized military hierarchy, eager to enter Europe, creeping up the Balkans to the very gates of Vienna until turned back, but like wolves, they could be heard howling the length of Europe's night. And in the middle of all this were the Russians, who throughout this era absorbed the full brunt of the Mongol attack, thereby protecting Europe, and who later on engaged in tireless battle with the Turks, again to the advantage of Europe.

A portrait of Peter the Great (1672–1725).

The East was regarded as in some way sinister as compared to the West, a prejudice which has lasted to this day in the popular European subconscious. And it was Russia's misfortune to lie in the East, and her motives were confused with all the nightmares emanating from that point of the compass. It was as though the European train was leaving the station towards a brighter technological and humanistic future, with Russia running along the platform seeking access to the moving carriages, only to be harassed by savage porters, and pushed off by high-minded Catholic dignitaries, Polish nobles, and Teutonic knights from the windows of their first class compartments.

The Russians fell back exhausted to wait for the next train, and to struggle endlessly with the others left stranded in the station. There was a relative lull after the 'Time of Troubles', a licking of wounds and a sharpening of claws. The restless frontiers continued to seethe as always, but it was not the moment for concentrated effort. There was too much to do at home, and despite the apprehensions of Europe, individuals still arrived in Russia in droves, eager to make their fortunes in a society short on technology and rich in rewards. The lure of Russia was not unlike the lure of America at a later date, which has been romanticized as the downtrodden and displaced longing for freedom. It was not always freedom which was the aim of its immigrants, but opportunity which was lacking in the highly exploited societies of their origins.

By the middle of the seventeenth century, only a little over three hundred years ago, the Russians had access to neither the Baltic nor the Black Sea, and Siberia was hardly tapped. The southern Russians, who had been detached from the north by the shock of the Tartar raids, now began to resist the Polish overlordship, and, eager to regain the autonomy which they always cherished, drifted eastwards again, while looking to the north. In 1654, the protectorate of the Tsar was acknowledged by the Ukrainian hetman Bogdan Khmelnitzki, and the rich land of the Ukraine was reincorporated into the Russian state, with the understanding that a Ukrainian national identity be preserved within the protective framework of the Russian state. This was an important date, since the violence of disruption had now been healed by a voluntary act of reunion. It goes without saying that a Polish war followed almost immediately in the wake of this agreement, and this time the reconstituted Russian army, with its foreign drillmasters, came out of the conflict rather better than on previous occasions, recapturing and holding various towns including the Russian city of Smolensk, and the ancient Lithuanian capital of Vilna. The Swedes prudently waited until the Russians were weakened by these victories to start another Swedish war, in which they did rather better than the Poles, retaking Livonia and Lithuania. But it was with internal developments that the interim period between the end of the Rurik dynasty and the arrival on the scene of Peter the Great was mainly concerned.

Bogdan Khmelnitzki freed the Ukraine from Polish domination and incorporated it into Russia while retaining its national identity.

We have already suggested that the Russian pendulum swings higher than that of other people, and there is also a curious tendency towards fundamentalism in the Russian soul, so powerful and so die-hard, that it inspires revolution and recklessness in its opponents. Naturally it is in religion that these currents are most clearly perceived, but they also extend into culture, and into daily life.

The patriarch Nikon, out of perfectly reasonable and conservative convictions, attempted to modernize certain aspects of the Orthodox belief, which were based on mistranslation and misconception of the scriptures, but he was immediately accused of sacrilege by those who regarded even errors as holy and above criticism. As the theological battle dragged on, some saw signs that the end of the world was nigh, and it is this prevailing superstition, and capacity for gratuitous mysticism, which goes some way to explain the virulence of the anti-clerical reaction of the Bolsheviks in the early revolutionary period, when they encouraged the Besbozhniki, or Movement of Godlessness.

Crowds were always moved much too easily for comfort by wild-eyed men whose lack of wholesome nourishment facilitated ectoplasmic visions in the sky, and it was not only the ignorant who were prey to the eloquence of witch doctors. We remember how the entire court of Nicholas II was under the influence of Rasputin, a hedonistic, woman-izing hulk of holiness, as insanitary in body as in mind. There the *Nostalgie de la Boue* was satisfied on Louis Quinze *canapés*, or with the oily hair stretched on starched pillows. Whole regiments of carefully groomed women seemed to relish this tumble from social grace, until a group of their habitual consorts got rid of the ruttish monk, giving him a protracted death as squalid as the adventure of his life.

Those who unswervingly followed the Old Beliefs were eventually excommunicated by the exasperated patriarch, suffering a more awesome fate than the recent followers of Archbishop Lefèvre, who, it will be remembered, refused to abandon the Latin mass, and were successively cajoled and threatened by a series of popes. Some of these unrepentant schismatics eventually found their way to Canada and the United States, where they still practice their ancient forms of worship to this day, together with the Dukhobors, who take their clothes off in public, and other obscure sects who practise self-castration, which is certainly a good reason for their obscurity.

It is significant that the Russian word for schism is *Raskol*, and that Dostoevsky, the most inspired of the speleologists who plunged into the caverns of the native spirit, called the protagonist of his novel *Crime and Punishment*, Raskolnikov. The symbolism makes the character of the young murderer with an overwhelming urge for redemption all the more interesting.

In a sense, the Church, apart from reformers like Nikon, and politi-cally enlightened prelates like Germogen, one of the principal engineers of an end to the troubles, represented a static element, which satisfied a great spiritual hunger, but harped as ever on traditional values, and frowned on questing thought as a positive danger to the process of thinking itself.

The clergy, and the princes of that clergy, did not differ greatly from their counterparts in other areas of Europe in their influence or manner, but few nations have ever suffered from an aristocracy as tenacious, obtuse and vindictive as the boyars.

At a period when kings were characterized as strong or weak, the great lords of every land jockeyed endlessly for position at the first hesitation of a monarch, but there was something unique about these boyars in a growing land with shifting borders. They behaved as members of some exclusive club, membership of which was based solely

In 1697 Peter the Great toured Western Europe. In Holland, Peter enlisted as a ship's carpenter in the shipbuilding centre of Zaandam. He lived in a cottage and took a local girl as his mistress.

on birthright. Within its walls, they poisoned each other's wine and chased the servants around the kitchen, and the only means of uniting them in a common purpose was not by invading their nation, but merely by applying for membership.

Ivan the Terrible, as a boy, left to stray aimlessly about his own palace in the clothes of a beggar boy, had memories of the boyars helping themselves to fistfuls of jewels from the national patrimony, and of sprawling on the royal bed with their boots on. They, too, represented a static element in the state, high priests of the status quo, hating each other in their hermetic exclusivity, and yet seeming to enjoy their hatred as blood sports are enjoyed by some. There must have been exceptions in the nature of things, but the atmosphere which members of this club exuded was retrogressive, vainglorious, and ponderous. They were kind of Sanhedrin created by heredity, feared by rulers and populace alike.

A catalyst which would bind the positive elements in the country into a cohesive, recognizable force, and at the same time would break through those barriers which held progress in check, was bound to come sooner or later. It came in the surprising shape of the fourteenth child of Tsar Alexei and his second wife.

Peter the Great was born within the walls of the Kremlin on 30 May 1672, and it soon became apparent that here was no ordinary child. First of all, his rate of growth was phenomenal. In maturity, he was only a whisker or two short of seven-foot tall. When he walked, others were forced to run to keep up with him. He had extraordinary energy, and applied it in all directions with rare intelligence.

The outset of his reign, however, was as unpromising as that of Ivan the Terrible had been. Nevertheless, whereas Ivan was only three years old at the time of his accession, Peter was ten, and looked much older. A boyar, Prince Vasili Golitsyn, became virtual regent. He was befriended by Sophia, an emancipated and conniving woman, aunt both to Peter and Ivan, his surviving half-brother, a seedy young man to whom the throne should have gone if the order of precedence had been observed. Sophia resolved to see Ivan on the throne, desiring the regency for herself. To this end, she began spreading rumours about Peter's mother and the venerable counsellor, Artamon Matveyev, suggesting that they were planning to do away with Ivan and betray the country to foreigners. There had been enough of this in the past to make these lies seem distinctly credible, especially to the Imperial bodyguard, the *streltsy*, or sharp-shooters, the praetorians of the Kremlin. However, rumours were not enough. At her behest, men galloped through the streets of Moscow proclaiming the terrible news. Matveyev and Natalya Naryshkina, Peter's mother, had had Ivan strangled!

Fearing that another time of trouble was well and truly launched, the *streltsy* rushed to the palace, followed by a gathering mob. Matveyev appeared on the balcony together with Natalya, Peter and Ivan. For a

ABOVE: Eighteenth-century view of St Petersburg from the River Neva
BELOW: Peterhof, built for Peter the Great in the eighteenth century

The young Tsars, Peter and Ivan, on twin thrones.

Gold coin showing Sophia of Russia, regent to the two young Tsars.

moment reason prevailed as Matveyev, with the authority and dignity of age, appealed to the sense of fair play of the *streltsy*, flattering them for their bravery. The day seemed to have been won for reason when young Prince Dolgoruky, whose ailing father commanded the *streltsy*, turned on them, upbraiding them for their gullibility and showering them with insults. This was too much for the soldiery, who lost their heads, tossing Dolgoruky onto the pikes of their comrades from the top of a staircase. Matveyev, wrenched from the arms of Natalya, suffered a similar fate. Ivan and Peter were left alone, but the incident had a marked effect on Peter, who learned at first hand, and brutally, the inconstancy of a crowd goaded by rhetoric and the disappearance of all judgment in moments of collective folly. It was a lesson he would never forget, and his face twitched occasionally for the rest of his life as a direct consequence of his introduction to the affairs of state.

Ivan and Peter shared the throne after that, prompted by Sophia, whose place was behind the curtains. She was only twenty-five years old herself, and a person of rare mettle. Not unnaturally, Peter was more than a match for his fragile half-brother, and began to dominate the proceedings. In 1687 and again in 1689, Golitsyn, Sophia's friend, led much heralded expeditions into the Crimea to attack the Turks, which were both markedly unsuccessful. Peter struck suddenly, as Ivan the Terrible had done before him, choosing this psychological moment to exile Golitsyn and bundle Sophia from her prompter's box behind the arras into a convent. He was then seventeen years old.

Attracted to sport, it looked as if this young colossus might yet develop into a feckless and capricious ruler. He spent a great deal of time in the so-called German suburb of Moscow, a kind of ghetto into which foreign specialists had been herded by Russian suspicion and prejudice, and where there was a perpetual intellectual ferment quite unlike the tone of the rest of the city. A Swiss expatriate, François Lefort, became his companion, and encouraged him not only in the pleasures of knowledge but also in the delights of the flesh.

The time soon came for Peter to try his hand at military adventure, and he led his own expedition against the Turks, which was hardly more successful than Golitsyn's had been. What he learned however, was important. He now had a measure of his own inadequacy, and on Lefort's advice, he took a most extraordinary initiative by any standards. He sent a mission to Western Europe to learn new military and naval techniques, and accompanied his own mission in the guise of an ordinary labourer.

His appetite for knowledge grew with learning. As a youth he had played at soldiers with his friends. He had divided them into the camps, and the boys then fired leather cannon-balls at each other. It was but a sketch of a dream, which needed filling out. Being of a temperament which enjoyed the thrills of discovery, and finding his mind wandering in the presence of tutors, he was largely self-taught. Although he only

A portrait medallion of Peter the Great

read and wrote with difficulty, he slowly acquired various techniques, including arithmetic. On a less ambitious level, he was an excellent carpenter, he knew how to print and work in both stone and metal, and could even draw teeth adequately. He also acquired an astrolabe, now in the Hermitage Museum, in a section dedicated to his achievements as a craftsman. This instrument, known to the ancients, but only recently rediscovered, permitted the user to calculate his latitude from the sky, and to tell the time of day. Rapidly his attraction for the sea grew, inculcated originally by a Dutch resident in the German suburb, Timmermann. He realized that there were methods by which ships could be induced to sail against the wind, and with these seemingly insignificant steps towards a full comprehension of British and Dutch mastery of sailing came the realization that power through trade was possible only with a mastery of the sea.

He travelled incognito to Germany and Holland, working for a while in a shipbuilding yard. He went to England, and stayed at Greenwich, where Ivan the Terrible's ambassadors had stayed. If it may be wondered how he could leave so turbulent a place as the Kremlin unattended for so long, the answer is that he was compelled to cut short his wanderings and hurry home to deal with new uprisings of the *streltsy*, directed by Sophia from her nunnery.

His problems were now at least as great as his ambitions. Somehow he had to make sense of his vast dominions, which by now stretched across

A nineteenth-century painting showing the execution of the *streltsy* at Peter the Great's order in 1698.

the bleak, bold face of Siberia, where the Cossacks, fleeing before the punitive forces of the Central Government, had reached the Pacific Ocean, or rather the Sea of Okhotsk as early as 1639.

To the north, the unexplored arctic lay under its forbidding cloak of snow and ice, with only Archangel as a seasonal port. To the south, the Turks blocked access to the sea, while to the west, there were still the old enemies.

The problems, Peter realized, were not merely military or economic. It needed a massive effort to improve the educational facilities, at first for the elite, later for everybody. Russia had to take an initiative in order not just to follow resentfully, and at a considerable distance, the innovative examples of smaller, better-organized nations. They had to have a society which was in some ways exportable, and not just be reliant on an endless, suspicious importation of influence from abroad.

The frame of this picture of Peter's nation had to be the sea. The sea is a civilizing influence. A shipwrecked sailor is rescued without being asked his nationality or religion before being hauled aboard. In its ugly moods, the sea is a common danger which unites all who sail it in a sense of fraternity. Not so the land, where every inflection of the countryside may conceal an ambush, and where ownership is mutely claimed by everything from ornamental gates to humble hedgerows, and from frontier posts to lines of inhospitable forts. And then, whoever heard of a goodwill division marching into a town?

If Russia was still backward, and illiterate, and often self-satisfied in its lugubrious condition, it was the land which was to blame, as it stretched like a carpet for thousands of ungovernable miles, but in no direction which really mattered strategically. From there had advanced all the unwelcome visitors, be they armed or not, coming to conquer or merely to exert their disruptive influence from the isolation of their ghettos. Russia, under boyars and Orthodox popes, wished to wallow in its own peculiar habits, its Russianness, undisturbed by novelty or other unhealthy concepts. Peter decided that it was time to open the windows of this vast, airless room.

He started by mobilizing every alien with even the slightest knowledge of ships and navigation. Peasants were dragooned into cutting down whole forests, and shaping the timbers into new and unexpected shapes. This improvised shipyard had to be inland, by force of circumstances. In a remarkably short time the new fleet was ready for action, and it left Voronezh for the south, down river, an incredible armada of men-of-war, fireships and support barges. It entered the fray at Azov to the immense surprise of the Turks, who thought they only had to deal with the seventy thousand foot-soldiers and horsemen they had dealt with on previous occasions. The town of Azov fell to Peter. The consequences were enormous. At last Russia had access to the Sea of Azov, which debouched into the Black Sea. The door was open, at least a crack.

A medal struck to commemorate the crowning of Catherine as Empress in 1724.

As the news, both surprising and alarming, spread through the courts of Europe, Peter sent another mission to the West, in order to test the possibilities of a Christian alliance against the Turkish infidel. The Turks were, in some quarters, regarded as more of an immediate menace than the Russians, and Peter expected a relative popularity after his exploit at Azov, but his suggestion met a cool reception. Nobody wished to provoke a sleeping dog, especially not in the company of one which seemed dangerously awake, and as ever unpredictable.

In fact, the belief demonstrated by the American leadership in recent years, that it is dangerous to give excessive technological aid to 'uncouth' peoples, since in the end it will be the hand of the donor which is bitten, was already rife at Peter's time. The huge embassy of over two hundred Russians, including a sailor called Mikhailov, who was none other but the Tsar in one of his numerous plebeian disguises, created an impression which would have been defined in present day Washington as 'counter-productive'.

There was, characteristically, considerable opposition within Russia to this mission, from people who feared contamination by the West of its members.

This attitude also has a modern parallel, often misunderstood by what is optimistically called 'the free world'. It is commonly believed that the seemingly hostile isolation of Soviet Embassy staffs or ballet companies, and the construction of such provocative obstacles as the famous Berlin wall is due to a general fear of downtrodden citizens attempting to escape. The occasional defection, or precipitate appearance of those who have managed to slip away from surveillance seems to prove this theory. But in fact this attitude has its origins in this same fear of contagion; a social system, which seems to a Russian on the highroad to Utopia, is threatened by infection from a fundamentally evil system: international capitalism. The Russian way of life, then and now, is to be regarded as a rare jewel worthy of protection, and if that protection entails discipline and a lack of the kind of frivolous freedom enjoyed elsewhere, that was and is a sacrifice well worth making. Politics had never really entered the consciousness of the ordinary Russian. He knows about conflict and intrigue. He knows about struggles for power. Whoever comes out on top is always respected until he or she misbehaves, when he is ejected. But the idea of representatives arguing in a prescribed building, in public, for all to see and hear, has never struck the Russians as being in any way reasonable or sensible.

If a person feels an urgent need for freedom, he can always go into the vast fields and forests, lie in the sun or roll in the snow, fish or shoot to his heart's content. That is freedom, but to spoil this fine bucolic feeling with extraneous matters like debate seems an adulteration of something beautiful with excruciating tedium and irrelevancy. Elections invariably lead to situations where almost half a nation is miserable and frustrated. Better, the Russians feel, for the whole of a people to be miserable or radiant at the same time. At least this is less divisive, and enables the populace to deal with the problems in a truly national and spontaneous manner.

Even if the Russians have only had a Duma, or State Parliament, for a very brief period in their history, it is peppered with *zemsky sobors*, *soviets*, and councils of all kinds. Russians have always been inveterate believers in the collegial administration of their own affairs, even during times of the most rigid autocracy. In such times, of course, the collectives became a conspiracy, but in debates of this nature, at least everyone concerned is on the same side, and they all know precisely the question at hand, even if they hold different opinions. Open argument, however, with the addition of loyalty to political parties, and fractions of parties, appears an utter waste of time, and a dangerous fanning of half-hidden fires, best extinguished in secret by those qualified to do so, be they the *streltsy* then, or the security police today.

Since the Russians know themselves to be placid by nature, but highly combustible when the temperature reaches a certain degree, they live in an aura of indifference, with a censorship which has always been the bane of artist and journalist alike, but which is on the whole approved by the populace as a buffer against undue excitement and provocation.

It is indicative that the word provocation is in wide use, and suggests invariably a sinister attempt to raise the temperature to a dangerous point, be it in personal or inter-governmental affairs.

Sailor 'Mikhailov' and his travelling circus entered Europe on the wave of naval success to sell the Russian view of the world as well as to learn. Shipbuilding was studied as well as gunnery and ballistics. These studies launched the great Russian artillery tradition. Since Peter planned internal waterways to link Russia's network of vast rivers, he also studied the craft of canal building, and encouraged even more foreigners to come and instruct his people. As far as the educational aspects of his mission were concerned, they could be counted a success, but it became clear that Russia had a long way to go before being taken seriously in the West. In fact, one tactless tongue was heard to mutter that this collection of solemn emissaries with beards and greasy locks cascading over their shoulders, were no more than baptized bears.

Part of Peter's Westernization programme included cutting off the beards of the boyars.

Another of Peter's reforms was the wearing of European clothes instead of Russian dress.

The remark must have rankled, because Peter began to regard the beard as a symbol of voluntary backwardness and patriarchal smugness. At the very moment of his return after an absence of a year and a half, he personally shaved the beards of countless boyars, and thereafter exacted a notorious tax on beards for those who still stubbornly clung to this outward sign of authority and wisdom. He also made it an offence to wear the flowing robes which had given noblemen their slightly nocturnal appearance, and induced them to adopt European dress. Small wonder that many besides the surviving Old Believers saw in Peter the anti-Christ they had all expected as a scourge for the sins of modernization. There is an interesting temperamental difference between the Jews and the Russians. The Jews, even in times of their greatest suffering, never ceased to expect the Messiah with the confirmation that their sacrifices had not been in vain. The Russians, even at moments of relative affluence and calm, expected the anti-Christ to punish them for the errors of their ways.

Peter was a supremely positive character, however, as all men with a mission are bound to be. He was not one to be influenced by the mumbo-jumbo of mysticism; in fact, he was determined to get rid of it once and for all. In that sense, he is still appreciated and lauded in the pragmatic

Russia of today, and there are always freshly cut flowers on his elaborate tomb in the chapel of the Peter and Paul Fortress in Leningrad, his city far more than that of Lenin. Who places them there is unknown, but they are never absent, and are always still alive.

The act of placing them there is a form of discipline, of which Peter would have approved, even if he would have shrugged off as superfluous the sentimental aspects of the continuing gesture. His initiatives were directed not only against the stubborn conservatism of the people, but against the lethargy which unventilated thinking produced. He forced the pace, as though attempting to keep his people busy. He tried to make them part of his personal evolution, and marshalled this basically indolent mass into some kind of army marching towards the sea and the cleansing gusts of fresher winds, which invigorate the body and clear the mind as they shatter the cobwebs of habit.

He concluded a peace treaty with the Turks now that he had a foot in the southern door, and immediately turned on Sweden, now the predominant bellicose power in the north. Whereas he had no success in finding allies against the Ottoman Empire, he acquired, for the first time

In 1700, Peter suffered a defeat at the hands of the Swedes at the battle of Narva.

in Russian history, allies in the West. That this was possible was entirely due to the expansionism of Charles XII of Sweden, whose armies were as redoubted as his ambitions were viewed with misgiving. Peter's allies in this conflict were Denmark and Poland, for once united with Russia in common resolve. This conflict lasted a full twenty years, and was pursued at enormous cost to all concerned.

It was during the early part of the war that the Russians occupied part of the Southern Baltic littoral, despite suffering a heavy defeat at the hands of the Swedes at Narva. Peter founded the city of St Petersburg on 1 May 1703, and the hut among the marshes where the idea of this great metropolis germinated still stands in all humility in the midst of splendid buildings as an embryo in a bottle. The broad river which gives the city its extraordinary proportions is called the Neva, as pretty a word as a girl's name, but which in Finnish means 'mud'. This is an indication of the absurd challenge presented by nature to the ever hopeful Tsar. It was, frankly, an impossible site to choose for a future capital, and thousands died among the bogs as they sought to lay the foundations. It was said later that the city was built on the bones of its creators. But still Peter pressed on with his Petropolis, a superb modern monument to his vision, swept by low scudding clouds and lashed by spray, a slap in the face to backward, slothful, dangerous Moscow which had caused him so much youthful misery.

Meanwhile, the Swedes had dealt effectively with both Danes and Poles, and turned their attentions to the remaining member of the coalition. King Charles's successes went to his head as Hitler's were to do after him, and mistrusting the tough nut of Moscow, he left it on his flank, and was attracted to the rich black soil of the Ukraine and the promises of gain beyond. His lines of communication became longer and longer on his precipitate march towards his destiny, but he was promised help by Mazeppa, the rebellious hetman of the Ukraine, a fact which gave him confidence. The help offered by Mazeppa turned out in reality to be no more than symbolic, and Peter, who had time to reorganize the Russian army yet again into a regional recruiting grid, each one of eight regions supplying and financing their own recruits instead of relying on that tiresome and above all slow centralization which had prevailed before, now stalked the cocksure Swedish king through the Russian southlands, and met him in Poltava on 27 June 1709. The result was the first great Russian victory since Azov, and before that since Kulikovo, against the Mongols. It was utterly decisive, the wounded Charles fleeing to Turkey, and his army scattered or captured. Russian troops restored the throne of Poland only six weeks later, and appeared in Pomerania in the vacuum created by the Swedes. As if that was not enough, the Russian fleet, liberated from its rivers, gained its first naval victory over the Swedes, a seafaring nation, at the Battle of Hango Cape.

Europe was impressed and chastened by the rapid development of the baptized bears since their return to captivity. With due regard for the rate at which news travelled in those days, the effect must have been somewhat commensurate with the extraordinary emergence of Japan two centuries later as a major industrial and military power after an existence entirely isolated from the influence of the rest of humanity.

Peter understood very quickly the rules of the marriage lottery which prevailed in Europe, a fascinating game of loveless betrothals for political ends which had formed and destroyed alliances, and altered frontiers since the end of the Roman Empire. Not since the tenth century, when the daughter of the Duke of Yaroslav of Kiev had married the son of Henri I of France, with other daughters given in marriage to Harald, King of Norway and Andrew, King of Hungary, had a Russian monarch been allowed access to the marriage stakes. And that was long ago, when Kiev was still a pristine dukedom, unaffected by the retrogressive burden of the Tartar invasions and three centuries of subsequent humiliation. Now Kiev was Russian, and Peter was a conqueror in his turn. With the help of his newly consecrated fleet, his armies had landed at Stockholm, ending Swedish military ambitions. With the coming of peace, Russia acquired Estonia, Livonia and parts of Finland, then, of course, Swedish. He was made Emperor. He married a niece to the Duke of Courland, and another to the Duke of Mecklenburg, which was the beginning of his interest in German affairs at the expense of his erstwhile allies, Denmark and Poland, in whom he lost interest now that Sweden had been vanquished.

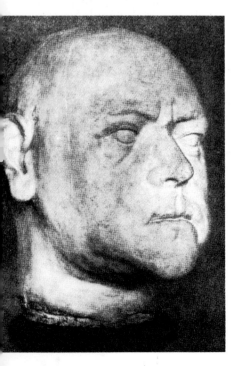

The face-mask of Peter made in 1719 while he was still alive.

He was, on the whole, less successful in dealing with the amorphous giant of Russia than he was in imposing his will on enemies. His temperament did not lend itself to the patient skills of organization which, by its nature, could not give dramatic or flamboyant results. The administration of this elephantine country would have taxed the ingenuity of even the most brilliant of European reformers faced with the impossibility of rapid communications and the high level of illiteracy throughout the population.

Peter tried everything. The Senate was the governing body, but he instituted so-called Colleges which functioned somewhat like Ministries do today; in order to coordinate the administration of certain specific works. There were those dedicated to Foreign Affairs, to the Army and to the Navy, as well as to Manufacture and Mining. There were others more vaguely named, such as a College of Revisions. The class of free and semi-free workmen were quickly crystallized into serfs, with their noble owners required to pay taxes on them, and the nobles themselves were made subject to obligatory service to the state. There were changes in local government all based on sometimes ill-digested and impractical concepts emanating from Germany and Sweden. But with all these efforts at simplification or streamlining, the tenuous chains of command became even more knotted, and the gloomy fact emerged that whatever

Peter the Great defeated the Swedes at the Battle of Poltava which marked the beginning of the rise of Russian dominance.

form these new solutions took, an enormous country required an enormous bureaucracy, a truth which has remained evident to this day. Corruption and inefficiency are inherent ingredients in the beehive of paperwork and misplaced zeal, especially when a large proportion of those responsible for its smooth functioning can neither read nor write. Peter, in his exasperation with the crushing expense of his campaigns and the morass which lay behind the lines, even promised handsome prizes for those who could come up with new ideas in the field of taxation, which was an eloquent commentary on the state of the new society.

His attention was drawn to both the ancient enemies of progress, the beardless boyars and the Church. He created a 'Holy Synod', yet another College dedicated to religious matters, thereby abolishing the Patriarchate and its authoritarian views on dogma. In other words, he democratized the Church by replacing the work of one man by the uncertainties of opinion. Naturally every initiative of this kind created its own latent opposition, its bitter resentment.

With all his activities, his prolonged absences, and his dedication to the future of an entire people, Peter could hardly be expected to be the ideal father. It was this neglect which proved to be his Achilles heel. He had made many if intermittent efforts to befriend his only surviving son, Alexis, but the boy was left for too long under the tutelage of the clergy, who inculcated in him an acute sense of his father's heresies, which

Peter the Great confronts his son, Alexis, at Peterhof after Alexis's forcible return from Vienna.

An engraving of the crowning of Catherine as Empress by Peter the Great

would sooner or later have to be expiated despite temporal successes. It was Alexis who humiliated his father by fleeing to Vienna, and placing himself under the protection of the Austrian Emperor as a political refugee, and this at a time when Russia's star shone bright in the international firmament for the first time. Protracted exchanges, some of them fraudulent and others degrading, eventually forced the young man's extradition. On his return, Peter's revenge was as thorough and unsentimental as all the positive aspects of his life had been. Locking his rancid hopes somewhere in the darkness of his heart, he had his only son tortured, and then compelled him to stand trial for treason. The judges, caught in an appalling trap between a sense of compassion for the tragedy of a family and what they deemed to be their duty, eventually passed sentence of death. The lad cheated the gallows by dying in his cell under circumstances which remain as enigmatic as the workings of Peter's mind.

He cheered himself up by remarrying in 1712 a Livonian domestic, Catherine Skavzonskaya, with whom he had been living for some time. She was a remarkable person by all accounts, as simple in manner as Peter, sharing his confidence and his bed, from which no fewer than eleven children saw the light. It was one thing for an Emperor to have even a prolonged adventure with an illiterate who compensated for her lack of culture in other ways, but it was quite another to crown her Empress. In a final flourish of defiance to the establishment, Peter did just that.

Perhaps feeling that his end was not far off, he decreed that in future a Tsar should personally designate his successor. With wonderful inconsistency he failed to do so himself, and he died as a consequence of an act as unkingly as it was human. He dived into the icy sea to rescue some sailors whose boat had overturned, and caught a cold which was to prove fatal. The sea which he had courted for so long at last responded to his advances.

CHAPTER SIX

Catherine the Great

The gap Peter left in the framework of the nation was enormous, and impossible to fill. There would have followed another time of troubles, but things were irrevocably different now. Even if the provinces remained somnolent, the life of the capital had changed, and the foreign influence was by now deeply ingrained in the nascent majesty of St Petersburg where it had been only grudgingly accepted by the battle-scarred and time-worn Moscow. Menshikov, Peter's lifelong crony from his youthful war games in the village of Preobrazhensky, the son of a stable hand, now seized the limp reins with a firm hand. Before anyone could react to his own advantage, Menshivkov, with the help of the Imperial Guard, who had replaced the notorious *strelsky*, proclaimed Catherine Empress, and Peter, the infant son of the dead Alexis, was conveniently sidetracked. But it did not last for long. During a smattering of short, characterless reigns, Peter II and Peter III passed in and out of sight like the saints of a Cathedral clock, to be followed by Anne, Peter the Great's niece, and not long thereafter by his daughter, Elizabeth.

There was nothing in any way remarkable about any of these brief reigns, except that there was a sudden emphasis on Western niceties, which fitted into the splendid buildings with which Italian and Scottish architects, together with a few gifted Russians, were beginning to embellish St Petersburg. A school for etiquette was opened, as well as one for ballroom dancing. Such events might have passed unnoticed in other European capitals, but in Russia they were of national importance. Of perhaps more durable value, a national theatre was created, an opera, for which the first of a long line of Italian directors was appointed, and, in 1755, the first university opened its doors, the dream of a man with a superbly questing mind, Lomonosov, poet and man of science. He had been born in the far north, where his father had been an Arctic fisherman. He was intended to follow in his father's footsteps, but a desire for learning quite as passionate but rather less brash than that which had obsessed Peter the Great, drove him to Moscow and from there to St Petersburg. He was selected as a member of that celebrated mission of Peter's, studying metallurgy among other disciplines, and beginning to write luminous verse. On an official level, he rose from Professor of Chemistry to Rector, and from there to Secretary of State. On an unofficial level, it was he who hewed a magnificently malleable language, full of subtlety and power of allusion from the two basic elements of the ancient ecclesiastical Slavonic, with its rigid neo-Hellenic syntax, and the loose, vulgar colloquial Russian of the people.

What this demonstrated, perhaps above all else, was that despite the

Peter the Great on his deathbed

mildewed civil administration and the imposition of an inflexible hierarchy based on class, it was already possible for a fisherman's son from the Arctic circle to rise to the heights of eminence if he had the talent and the will to do so.

The women who ruled Russia for a time were not without character, like the two Peters before them. Anne was a strapping creature with a short neck who liked shooting rifles and surrounded herself with Germans. This personal predilection led to her overthrow, and the installation of Elizabeth on the throne.

Elizabeth was a handsome woman, on a scale with her famous father, whom she resembled in character as well as in appearance, except that she never really abandoned the fecklessness of youth as he had done. Her paramour was a Sergeant of the Guard, and when she was encouraged to seize power, he was sent tongueless to Siberia to ruminate on his royal past, without being able to impart his secrets.

Russian troops put in their appearances at all sorts of minor foreign conflicts, but there was no gain of any kind from these demonstrations, only expense. And meanwhile the only real progress came in the fields of learning. On a more superficial level dancing became fashionable, manners more florid and costumes, at least of the wealthy, more elaborate. Elizabeth is reputed to have had upwards of fifteen thousand of these, scattered in the various Imperial cupboards.

Only in one respect did she do better than her father, and that was in selecting with the greatest possible care the successor to this difficult throne. Her desire was to favour the line of her sister Anne, who had become Duchess of Holstein. There was a son from this union, called Peter in deference to his famous grandfather, but born a Lutheran. Now the young man was invited to St Petersburg to be groomed as a future Tsar, and to adapt himself to Orthodoxy and other Russian ways. He accepted the invitation, and married a not very attractive, and certainly not very rich German princess, Sophie of Anhalt-Zerbst. The marriage was disastrous for the couple, but was destined to be a great success for Russia.

The idea of being Empress one day excited Sophie enormously, and she overrode the misgivings of her parents, who regarded the whole project as a kind of exile. But Sophie was extraordinarily thorough as well as headstrong. She plunged into the Imperial adventure with a missionary spirit, determined that nothing would stand in the way of her success at her job. Hers was an essentially Germanic temperament, and it was to prove sufficiently unusual in the highest echelons of the Russian court to be enormously beneficial. Actually it had been Frederick the Great of Prussia who had tipped Elizabeth in the young woman's favour since he saw Russia as a potentially dangerous enemy, and wished to keep his influence at the Russian court.

Both Sophie and her husband became converts to the Orthodox faith, he reluctantly, she avidly. Very quickly, his aversion to all things Russian grew to manic proportions, and seemed to retard his development as a person. His nostalgia for Prussian drill was such that he would load the bed with toy soldiers, and imagine great campaigns on the eiderdown, presumingly using his recumbent wife as nothing more than undulations in the landscape. She would certainly spend half the night cramming Russian grammar from a pile of books. The more he reverted into the petulance of childhood, the more she developed into a formidable expert in all things Russian. She even changed her name from Sophie, which was reminiscent of that other Sophie of evil memory, to Catherine. (It was the erosion of time which was to give her another name, in every way equal to the mighty forebear of her dilapidated husband, 'the Great'.)

Catherine (1729–96) as a young woman.

LEFT: Count Gregory Orlov, Catherine's lover and the murderer of her husband, Peter III.

When Elizabeth died, Peter III embarrassed all and sundry by his behaviour at her funeral, while Catherine behaved with the greatest propriety under her canopy of funeral veils. Peter lasted six foolish months, importing Holsteiners by the dozen to slake his nostalgia for his native land, and intending to help the little Dukedom with Russian soldiers in order to snatch a few acres of land from Denmark. This, and other evidence of his total lack of judgment was enough to drive the court to distraction. The only remote sign of judgment he ever showed was when Catherine was brought to bed with a child of unknown paternity, he acknowledged it as his own, perhaps with some relief. Catherine, despite her somewhat formidable appearance – she looked more like a slightly effeminate man than a woman – seems to have possessed extraordinary powers in the bedchamber, now that the tin divisions had been returned to their boxes. At the time of her husband's short rule, her lover was a Count Orlov, an officer in the Preobrazhensky Regiment of Guards. He and his brother engineered the downfall of Peter III while he was absent from court inspecting his beloved Holsteiners. Catherine was acclaimed Empress and installed in the Winter Palace before Peter had time to appeal for loyalty. On hearing of his wife's public infidelity, Peter crumbled, and begged to be able to emigrate to his beloved flatlands of Holstein. Before he could be answered, the Orlovs reported to the new Empress that her husband was dead 'in a quarrel', which was tantamount to the celebrated formula of dictatorships, 'while trying to escape'.

RIGHT: Gregory and his brother, Alexei. It is believed that the killing was actually carried out for Gregory by Alexei.

It was against this background that Catherine entered the Age of Reason, launching correspondences with celebrated international figures like Voltaire and Diderot, as well as with fellow monarchs such as Frederick the Great and Maria Theresa of Austria-Hungary. She was as meticulous with her pen as she was prodigal with her body. She even wrote some ambitious plays, 'En imitation de Shakespeare', as the flyleaf announced. They were mercifully short, yet introduced hundreds of characters from Russia's murky past, who were to parade before the spectator in incredible profusion, utilizing archaic language in the service of the imagined protocol of long ago. There was not much action despite a gathering glut of corpses, and they showed that perhaps because of the Germanic thoroughness with which she savaged every problem that came her way, the nature of Shakespeare's genius eluded her utterly. Shakespeare could have made a splendid banquet of Russian history had he known about it, for all his favourite elements are there: terror, compassion, comedy both high and low, introspection, remorse, the pleasure of cruelty, the strength of weakness, the weakness of strength, the paradox of power. She could reflect none of these. All she saw in Shakespeare was pomp and heraldry.

Unlike Peter the Great, she did not have to learn about European ideas. They came to her naturally. And she was clever enough in dealing with her Russian Counsellors not to insist if she felt she was opposed. Historically used, as they were, to autocracy and all its attendant follies, they were impressed by the soft breeze of liberality which was allowed to flow in their meetings with her.

It was perhaps also the fact of being German which attracted her to the Latin temperament, in which she saw a lightness and objectivity denied her countrymen. The functional Bibles of her reforms were *The Spirit of Law* by the Frenchman Montesquieu, and *Crimes and Punishments* by the Italian, Beccaria. She put forward revolutionary hypotheses, certainly heard for the first time in Russia, if not elsewhere, such as that all men were equal under law, that freedom was the right to do anything not specifically forbidden by law, that torture should be abolished, and that a jury system should include peasants among the judges. She maintained that the purpose of law was the prevention of crime, and not its punishment and prescribed a limitation of serfdom, and the restriction of large estates.

Not unnaturally there was an immediate opposition to such ideas, and Catherine did not insist. The project was against the interests of practically everyone who could read it. Those who could not were not in the habit of being consulted. And yet the very fact that such reforms could even be suggested, and by a monarch at that, was of enormous historical importance since it marked the first influence of foreign social ideas as opposed to mere techniques, and even while being rejected they sowed seeds for the future.

Turkish Bath in the Ekaterinsky Palace, which was built by Catherine the Great. It is an expression of the grace and elegance which she brought to her reign.

The flexibility of Catherine in her dealings with the aristocracy turned her long reign into a golden era for them. She laid great emphasis on creating elegance in her new capital of St Petersburg, now more isolated by the dismal distances of Empire than ever. It was a showpiece, the Brasilia of the epoch, constructed like a pavilion in some glorious world fair rather than as a habitable city. There was everything to delight the senses, and a sizeable foreign element to make the atmosphere cosmopolitan, and conversation stimulating. But the figurehead had little to do with the ship. Moscow, like a discarded mistress, had reverted to being a large provincial city in the heartland of the country, as it had been in landlocked times, with memories of the tormented past, and irremovable battle scars.

Thwarted for the time being in her administrative ambitions, Catherine looked outward, the time-honoured reflex of those with internal dissent on their hands. Profiting from the antagonism between her two most influential rivals in Eastern Europe, Prussia and Austria, she resolved to go further than Peter the Great had done on her southern border, and went to war with Turkey, supported by the Prussians, but opposed by the Austrians. Her armies under Rumiantsev won a victory over the Turks in 1774, and the right to be acknowledged protector of the Christian minorities within the borders of the Ottoman Empire, an important moral concession.

Frederick the Great then proposed, somewhat cynically, that between them Russia and Prussia should make a meal of the much diminished kingdom of Poland, sandwiched uneasily between the two. He suggested slyly that such acquisition might compensate Russia for the heavy expenditure during the Turkish war. This carniverous act brought Russia and Prussia into direct contact, and the outbreak of the second Turkish war found Russia in alliance with Austria and opposed to Prussia. This time she conquered the wide steppe between the Dnieper and Bug rivers, thanks to her commanders Repnin and Suvorov. Then, while both Prussia and Austria were unexpectedly engaged on their western borders with the French Revolutionary wars, she helped herself to a second portion of Poland, installing a favourite as king of that now unhappy land.

The Russian army had become one to be reckoned with. Its strength was, as always, the stubbornness and fatalism of its men, but by now it had officers of experience, and at least one of genius. Field Marshal Suvorov was a small man, only a little taller than a dwarf, but with a will and determination second to none. He was already old at the time, but if he had been a little younger, the course of the Napoleonic Wars might well have taken a different turn. His orders of the day were always a model of succinctness, such as 'The enemy will be taken prisoner', so that everyone knew what they had to do.

At times, owing to the exigencies of the awkward alliances against

A family group showing Catherine, her husband Peter III and son, Paul.

Emelyan Pugachev in a cage after his capture.

Napoleon, Suvorov was subjected to the overall command of conventionally-minded Austrian generals like Mack, but when he could escape from these strictures, he won every action he engaged in, culminating in the extraordinary crossing of the gorge near the St Gotthard pass in Switzerland, when an entire Russian army evaded a French trap by making a bridge of their belts, and passing even pieces of artillery across a raging torrent. There is to this day a memorial on the St Gotthard pass, gold letters on a black marble, in the Cyrillic alphabet, recording the extraordinary event. No less an authority than Nelson held Suvorov in the greatest esteem, and he appealed to Byron's romantic nature.

However, military exploits were not enough to offset the renewed stagnation of rural life. Behind the façade of palaces and intellectual badinage lay that same old, unsettled wilderness of human beings who had hardly moved technically or emotionally since the first Mongol invaders disturbed their peace. In some senses, they had regressed, since the old tribal freedoms had been replaced by serfdom and a bureaucracy of a kind decided their fates. Now there came a hideous reminder of the 'Time of Troubles' to shake the refined grace of St Petersburg. Far in the hinterland, a Cossack, by name of Emelyan Pugachev, had the bright idea of proclaiming that he was, in fact, Peter III, who had never died, but merely gone into hiding. As in the case of the false Dmitris nearly two centuries before, he was immediately believed by those whose lives lacked excitement, especially when he announced his intention of freeing the serfs. The systematic torture and murder of landowners began, their houses were burned to the ground, merchants and priests were not spared. Thousands flocked to his banner, including many members of minorities acquired by Russia in her expansion northward and southward. The rebellion acquired gigantic proportions, and was put down with the greatest of difficulty. Pugachev was ultimately captured, caged, and executed in the Red Square in Moscow. It is interesting that the execution took place in Moscow, the city of echoes, and not in St Petersburg, whose virginity was not desecrated by a sight of such ancient vulgarity.

The uprising took place in 1773, and although it was a kind of replay of what had been the rule in 1610, it still forestalled the French Revolution by a handful of years. Insurrection was in the air. Catherine had another shot at reform to accommodate these tendencies, and to keep the river of progress moving instead of allowing it to gather into stagnant pools. In 1775 she produced her Statute of Provinces, now no longer

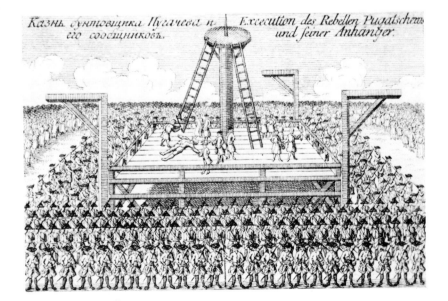

The execution of Pugachev in Red Square, Moscow in 1775

Catherine the Great in old age

influenced by the generalities of Montesquieu, but by the more palpable
administrative ideas of her adviser, Sievers. The idea was to decentralize
local government by making it responsible for its own judiciary
finances and administration, the only sensible course in a country as
huge. Councils of provincial nobles were to meet every three years to
discuss regional matters and elect their own 'Marshals of Nobility', the
secretaries of their clubs. On another level, a charter for burgesses laid

the foundation for the first real local government in Russia, separated from the activities of the nobles. Although it did nothing to alleviate the dissatisfaction of the serfs, it was a considerable advance along the road to efficiency.

As is so often the case, however, the liberal tendencies in Catherine were cut short by the outbreak of something far more drastic, which drove her into a posture of quite uncharacteristic reaction. The outbreak of revolution in France scared all the crowned heads of Europe, especially when Louis XVI and Marie Antoinette were beheaded. The writings of intellectuals, so agreeable to discuss during candlelit dinners as abstract ideas, had suddenly crystallized into violent and ugly reality. Unlike the emotional rebellion of Pugachev, which had taken place far from the nerve-centre of power, the intellectual revolution was centered in Paris, and the head of France was seized. Without the head, the body was impotent. The swiftness of it all, and the thoroughness, dismayed all royal observers, as though they realized that there was no road back into a more comfortable history. From that moment on, the game had to be played according to different rules.

Since Marie Antoinette was an Austrian princess, Austria and other powers tried to intervene militarily, only to be thoroughly thrashed by the French revolutionary army, now fired with new proletarian ideas.

Catherine was as deeply shocked by these events as any other monarch, even if she did profit by the distractions they caused to snitch another bit of Poland. She refused to allow the tricolor flag of the French republic to fly in the harbour of St Petersburg, and she began a personal persecution of those liberals she had herself encouraged. The Russian novelist, Radischev, the author of a book which had found favour previously, was sentenced to death as a 'Jacobin' in 1790, a time whose novelty was adapted to circumstances in a most marked way. He was lucky, for his sentence was commuted to ten years in Siberia. When he came home Napoleon was already in command of the tarnished dream.

When Catherine died after a reign of thirty-four years, she left behind a nation which to all intents and purposes occupied that one-sixth of the earth's surface which it occupies today. She was Empress in a period marked by grace and manner and intellectual ferment. It was also a period of libertines, during which fear of hellfire was more than compensated by the subtle delights of the flesh. The sweet condiment of hypocrisy was added to the vocabulary of the rake, and the confusion and elaborate pleading of the victim constituted half the joy of the chase.

Catherine was a stranger to none of this, and learned the moves of her times as thoroughly as she had learned the canons of the Orthodox Faith and the Russian language. Her bedchamber was rarely a place for solitary reflection. She lived to the full, and obeyed the rules of procedure whether dressed in mourning for those she did not care for or undressed in deference to those she cared for a great deal.

CHAPTER SEVEN

The Struggle with Napoleon

And she left a legitimate heir, whose instability and absurdly contemptuous appearance did indeed proclaim him to be the son of Peter III. His name was Paul, and he was hardly an improvement on his father, who had decreed that nobles should be free to hunt in the streets of St Petersburg. It was never made quite clear what they were permitted to hunt there. Paul had a charming palace which Catherine built for him at Pavlovsk, and a statue of him stands in the forecourt. It is as a sculpture as perspicacious in its cruelty as some of Goya's portraits of royalty. His pug nose raised above a characteristic simper gave him a remarkably fatuous appearance, while the stance of his body is a wonderful mixture of affectation and arrogance.

He was, in fact, quite as lunatic as his father had been, except that he preferred treating real soldiers as though they were made of tin to treating tin soldiers as though they were real. This was a step towards the strait jacket. His internal policy was as arbitrary as his mother's had been consistent. On the one hand he reduced the serfs' obligation to work for their masters to a three-day week, which sounds like a trades unionist's pipe dream, but on the other hand he turned many free peasants into serfs in order to please the nobility. But he had none of his mother's *savoir faire* or resilience, and his intelligence was always marred by an almost comic belief in the divine right of hereditary monarchs. In fact, he changed Peter the Great's instructions about the choice of the next Tsar by the incumbent, and decreed that the succession should once again be regulated by heredity. Perhaps it was because he only became ruler when he was well into middle age that the infantilism demonstrated by his father took on a more developed, and therefore more sinister form.

Whereas his father had, on one occasion, during his war games, caught a rat scurrying among his tin regiments like some secret weapon, had it court-martialled for insubordination, and hanged by the neck, toys were to be found in reality. He seriously believed that only conversation with his royal self conferred any degree of importance on anyone at all.

By the time he was on the throne, the beacon of the French revolution had burned itself out. Napoleon, at first Proconsul, then self-crowned Emperor, had now re-established France's reputation among the other crowned heads as a parvenu, perhaps, but at least as a crowned parvenu, and as such, one who accepted the principles of the game even if he had tampered with the rules.

The last act of Paul's reign was to plot with this inspired upstart to send a joint expeditionary force to India, and drive the British out.

It never came to anything, since Paul was murdered in his palace by a group of conspirators led by Count Pahlen, and perhaps not entirely

A painting of Emperor Paul I (1754–1801) by V. L. Borovikovsky.

without the knowledge of his son, Alexander I, one of the most intriguing and complicated characters in the whole of Russian history.

A favourite of his grandmother's, and physically as handsome as his father had been repellent, Alexander was always groomed by Catherine in the hope that he would become Tsar instead of Paul. Catherine, never insensitive to appearance, spent long hours instructing the young man in the secrets of being a Tsar, and he was deeply impressed by her opinions, and attempted, from the outset of his reign, to emulate her, and to ask himself what she would have done under any given circumstances. He immediately endeared himself to the liberal elements in his entourage by speaking with evident feeling about the barbarism of his nation, a state which he attributed to the traffic in human beings. He took certain peremptory steps, which were the evident consequence of his personal assessment of the situation, and not just transitory follies. He expressly forbade the use of torture in the cross-examination of suspects, (shades of Catherine's first and unsuccessful attempts at reform?). He proclaimed an amnesty for political prisoners. He even abolished the secret police. He encouraged the printing of books, both foreign and Russian, and permitted foreign travel without elaborate permission. Finally he was responsible in inducing Mikhail Speransky, the son of a simple village priest, and one of the most outstanding minds in Russia, to draft a new constitution. The result was a surprising and praiseworthy leap forward towards a form of representational government, right down to, and including the peasants, if not yet the serfs.

His intimates advised him of the dangers of a premature liberation of the serfs, although many seemed to agree that such a vital gesture would be inevitable in the future. A compromise was reached in 1803, when an *ukaze* permitted landowners to free their serfs if they felt so inclined while granting them lots of their own. Under 50,000 serfs were freed in this manner.

It was recognized by Alexander that the basis of all reform lay in literacy, and basic culture. He did his utmost to encourage this, and three new universities date from the early part of his reign.

In view of the historic tendencies of Russian monarchs, and the manner in which the nature of their position went to their heads in some way or other, for better, or usually for worse, Alexander's disposition at the outset was almost unbelievably rational and clement. His refinement of manner and great interest in matters of state seemed to preserve him from undue influence, and yet it was noticed by some that when he was not inclined to reach a decision about a given subject, he would mutter something inconclusive and drift into some other topic. If cornered, he could give way to his temper, but on the whole he maintained an opaque exterior to the world, as if he had things on his mind which were of more immediate concern than the matter which had been brought to his attention. To some his rather abstract personality seemed to mask a

Catherine the Great, Empress of All the Russias.

inherent weakness of character, while to others his was a temperament which could not be rushed, as though his intelligence needed time to control and censor the impulses of his nature.

The truth about this may have been found out had his reign continued untroubled by exterior problems, but these now clouded the issue, with the beginning of Napoleon's restless marches and countermarches across the face of Europe.

Alexander, on purely moral grounds, decided that Napoleon was a blight which had to be resisted at all costs if civilization were not to be irreversibly contaminated. This upstart, who had waited for the revolution to lose its voice with shouting and its energy with the wounds it inflicted on itself, suddenly replaced the symbols of popular power with those of Empire, and seized the crown from the hands of a surprised Pope in order to crown himself. He was thus not a figure calculated to endear himself to the enlightened reformer. Already Beethoven had torn up the dedication of the Eroica to his former hero, replacing it with a cutting epitaph to the 'Memory of a Great Man'. Now it was Alexander's turn. He had to make his gesture.

Despite the chronic economic difficulties at home, he pledged Russian armies to the coalition against Napoleon. There was no pressing need to enter an alliance at such a time, unless an extraordinary prescience be attributed to Alexander, which is somehow difficult to credit. It was more likely he was tempted to war by high moral principles, which more recent history shows to be a tenuous argument for conflict, and even in many cases, an open invitation to disaster.

If Russian armies were defeated by Napoleon's genius, which extended both to strategy and tactics, they were not disgraced. They probably even benefited from the experience as the great campaign of 1812 which was destined to follow showed. At Austerlitz in December 1805, while subordinated to the effete and conventional direction of Austrian commanders, and at Friedland, where the Russians were on their own, they acquitted themselves well, although suffering heavy losses. The alliance between Russia, Austria, England and Sweden was designed to rid Northern Europe of Napoleon's 'Continental System'. This was a blockade of Britain and a forerunner of Hitler's notorious new order in Europe. Like Hitler after him, Napoleon planned to make Europe one imperial state from which the arch enemy, England, would be excluded.

However, in 1807 Napoleon met Alexander on a barge at Tilsit, a symbolic meeting place which it must have taxed the talents of the chiefs of protocol to devise. Napoleon was able to use all his suave charm and Gallic objectivity on the fundamentally shy, idealistic, and vulnerable Alexander, who had already been influenced in his youth by the Swiss republican, LaHarpe. Napoleon, the ape of contemporary caricature, and the bogey man of Europe, turned out, as so often happens, to be a

Alexander I (1777–1825), painted by F. P. Gérard.

The meeting of Napoleon and Alexander I on the barge at Tilsit in 1807.

rational, jocular, and even agreeable man despite the charisma which his achievements and attitude spread before him. Alexander, ever conscious of being the Emperor of a major power, evidently conquered his inhibitions to the extent of showing off, and even ranting about the subjects closest to his heart. At all events, Napoleon referred to him in retrospect as a 'Northern Talma', Talma being his favourite tragedian on the Parisian boards. The French Emperor must have spent the time in which he was not using his powers of persuasion as a spectator of quite a performance. The performer must have been grateful for his reception by the audience of one, for what transpired from this brief aquatic interlude was a somewhat emotional treaty of eternal friendship, which freed Alexander to attack the Swedes, and to contribute to the blockade of England. The virtue of this eternal friendship, in the eyes of Europe, was that it did not last very long. Although Finland was annexed in 1809, and Bessarabia was captured from the Turks in the fateful year of 1812, relations between France and Russia could hardly have been called a model of mutual trust.

Alexander and Napoleon met again in 1808, at a new summit conference a year after the first one. This time it took place on terra firma, at Erfurt in Germany, and neither the performance of the 'Northern

Talma' nor the applause of the single spectator seem to have reached the heights a second time. The meeting had neither the freshness nor the elaborate preparation of the previous encounter, and both men had cause for irritation, and consequently saw each other in a newer, truer light.

Napoleon, who had espoused the cause of the Polish exiles in France, many of them gallant cavalry men who had fought with enviable panache in the Peninsular Wars and elsewhere, now raised the entire Polish question with Alexander and met a sullen silence. (The pale, slender shadow of President Reagan is but a reminder of past coolness.) Napoleon, as a recent recruit to the ranks of emperors, had done his homework well as regards the role of marriage in the field of politics, and now also demanded Alexander's sister's hand, an act of generosity which would have given the necessary security to the protestations of eternal friendship. Alexander was obdurate in his refusal. In fact, the tragedian of a year ago hardly seems to have given a performance on this occasion. The clamour came from the auditorium, and the day ended in an atmosphere of high tension.

The Diet at Porvoo in 1809 confirmed the annexation of Finland by Russia.

The initial treaty had occasioned much opposition within Russia, and the nobility, as ever conscious of the length and purity of its lineage, reacted strongly against any truck with an ambitious Corsican corporal. This attitude was enough to strengthen Alexander's hand, and to make him impervious to Napoleon's ability as a negotiator.

Alexander, it would seem, was a most eloquent example of the intense desire of certain men to remain themselves despite the high office they hold, a hope which is virtually impossible in the nature of things, owing to the unnatural pressures and political expediencies which place that cherished simplicity under continual assault. Ironic, even humorous in private, (he called his close associates, who helped him formulate his early attempts at reform, his 'Committee of Public Safety', after the French revolutionary government), he was yet capable of astonishing outbursts of autocratic megalomania when cornered by an unanswerable argument, or a contradiction in his own utterances, ('I am the autocratic Emperor, and I will this, and nothing else!').

Before he entered into his treaty with Napoleon, with the battles of Austerlitz and Friedland as yet unfought, his mind, uninfluenced by the pain of gruff reality, had conceived a plan for peace which is remarkable even by the standards of a modern world, whose excruciating suffering in two world wars and the presence of arsenals of nuclear weapons in its hedgerows and under the surface of its waters, has rendered it open to the idealism of the last ditch.

He wished to ensure that the sacred rights of humanity be preserved by making governments incapable of action, save in the greatest interest of their subjects. To this end, he proposed that the relations of states with one another should be regulated according to more binding rules. He urged states to accept that it would be in their own interest to respect these rules. He believed that this was possible if a European Confederation could be created, based on clear principles of the rights of nations. 'Why could one not submit to it?' the Tsar wrote to his ambassador in London. 'The positive rights of nations assure the privilege of neutrality, insert the obligation of never beginning war until all the resources which the mediation of a third party could offer have been exhausted, having by this means brought to light the respective grievances, and tried to remove them? It is on such principles as these that one could proceed to a general pacification, and give birth to a league of which the stipulations would form, so to speak, a new code of the law of nations, which, sanctioned by the greater part of the nations of Europe, would without difficulty become the immutable rule of the cabinets, while those who should try to infringe it would risk bringing upon themselves the forces of the new union.'

This astonishing document was penned by Alexander, alone at his desk, the man who had access to his own mind in the solitude of his own company. It reads like a premature paean to the United Nations, not

'The journey of a great traveller'. A caricature of Napoleon's flight from Moscow.

written by some theorist without the means to do more than dream on paper, but by the ruler of one of the most powerful nations in the world.

It is evident that a mind as clairvoyant as this was a permanent prey to the horrid exigencies of the daily round, the endless compromises due to the state of the nations, its divergent mentalities, to say nothing of the endless fluctuations of foreign policy. An autocrat he may have been by law, but he was neither stupid nor insensitive enough to take advantage of the fact. He was that most unfortunate of men, a rebel in a situation of authority. But, as other Tsars had shown, to have authority over a land mass as raw and as amorphous as Russia was to be, at times, as helpless as a serf.

The result of his accommodation with Napoleon was to prove disastrous. The famous Continental System did not work, and the Russian economy suffered from its effects. An acrimonious correspondence began between Napoleon and Alexander. Alexander, spared a physical contact with Napoleon, could more than hold his own on paper.

Napoleon realized that here was an adversary whom he could convert rapidly to his point of view at a conference, but who reverted to his original platform when the excitement of a personal confrontation had given way to reflection. He referred to Alexander as a 'Sly Byzantine', which was about as offensive as a Mediterranean self-made man could get, and in 1812 he replaced social graces with military action.

The invasion of Russia was to be the final consecration of Napoleon's reign, a swift and terrible retribution after time wasted in parley and enticement. The *Grande Armée* was between two and three times as powerful as the Russian regulars, and immensely impressive despite its reliance on foreign levies, troops from various German principalities, and the indomitable Poles. The advance, at the beginning, went according to plan, the Russians, under a general of Scottish origin, Barclay de Tolly, retiring in order before the French, refusing open battle. This policy came in for some criticism, and Barclay was replaced by a general admirably suited to the occasion not only by his curious temperament, but by his indisputable Russianness. Field Marshal Kutusov only had one eye, but the other was unusually perspicacious, even though it frequently closed in sleep. By his own admission, this hugely corpulent old man used to pretend to sleep in order the better to hear the opinions of his *aides-de-camp*. Whether this was true or not, or merely a clever excuse for his unusual somnolence even under the most drastic circumstances, will never be known, but it served to increase his mystery.

He stood firm on the field of Borodino, more or less under pressure of patriotic opinion, for this was rapidly disintegrating into the first great total war in history. The battle was terrible, and inconclusive. Both sides suffered enormous losses, but try as he might, Napoleon could not make it decisive. Kutusov refused to fall into any of the traps which were set for him.

The burning of Moscow, 1812. A contemporary illustration.

After the battle, the Russians continued their slow, \
drawal, while the French were harassed by civilians and C \
manders. Everywhere they advanced, they met voluntary d \
burning houses and fields. The policy known as 'Scorched Eart. was in operation for the first time. There was no succour, no foodstuffs, anywhere. Moscow was abandoned. Napoleon entered its empty streets, unapplauded, only the clatter of hooves resounding in the utter inhospitability. Then a smell of burning spread, and soon great flames could be seen leaping above the silhouettes of the buildings. Rostopchin, the mayor, had given the order for the burning of Moscow. It was his visiting-card, presented to the French Emperor according to the etiquette of the day.

Napoleon brooded and fretted for a week in this carcass of a city, feeling that the rules of civilized warfare had been somehow desecrated by this act of barbaric defiance. He had counted on being able to feed his army off the land. Even that elementary decency had been denied him.

On only the eighth day of his hollow victory, he debased himself by writing to Alexander in St Petersburg, admitting the plight of his magnificent army, and begging Alexander to respect 'even the remnants of former sentiments'.

Alexander replied with a categoric refusal. 'No more peace with Napoleon!'

And yet, a part of Alexander's sensitive spirit had been broken by the enormity of the events which had struck his country, and for which he searched his soul for traces of responsibility.

As so often happens with men who are only really themselves when alone, he found this necessary solitude too heavy a burden under the awful circumstances of his destiny. The nightmare of Napoleon's retreat under the falling snow, forced to take the same way out as he had taken in by the vigilant and intact armies of Kutusov, marching on a road parallel to his own, led to one of the most complete and satisfying victories of all time.

The French and their allies were utterly routed, although the Russians could have destroyed the *Grande Armée* to practically the last man if there had not been a *mésentente* between Tormagov's Cossacks and the main body of the Russian forces. When Kutusov was questioned about this gaffe by a French prisoner of war, the wily old warrior is supposed to have replied that the error was deliberate. When pressed further by the incredulous Frenchman, Kutusov is alleged to have asked the question, 'Why destroy the French army?' And then added, 'To let the British into Europe?'

This may be the truth, or only Kutusov's remaining eye at work. It has the ring of possibility if not of truth. Victory left Alexander with the aura of a conqueror, the last flattery which his fragile spirit needed. He was now compelled to appear at conferences and congresses, not as a man searching for his truth despite his position, but as a monarch crowned by glory and the adulation of the civilized world. He took refuge in the consolation of religion, as many have when confined to cells, or indeed to palaces. For a king, a palace is a kind of prison. Without changing his ideas radically, the arteries of his mind hardened perceptibly. He corresponded with evangelical leaders, seeking solace for his soul's perplexities. To one of them, he confided that the fires of Moscow had illuminated his soul, 'I then got to know God and became another man.'

A lady from Basle, Frau von Krüdener, and another Swiss, Emparytaz, became his confidants, and shared his anguish with the sweet smiles of professional evangelism. Indeed this parochial atmosphere, with its unswervable convictions expressed with all the pious simplicity of which such people are capable, the penetrating yet kindly eyes aglow with a superior knowledge, all these must have seemed a relief to Alexander after the more theatrical, ornamental rituals of Orthodoxy, with its stifling incense, and more remote and formal appeals to the Almighty. They had prayer meetings all the way to Paris and Napoleon's final undoing, singing hymns, probably in unison.

At the Congress of Vienna, Alexander had to perform again, the part of kingship which he was least equipped for. Not for the first, and certainly not for the last time in history, did the sceptical West suspect the Russians of insincerity, and underhand designs. Metternich, a man not notable for his openness to ideas outside a bailiwick he knew and felt at home in, was irritated by the exalted 'language of evangelical abnegation', which to him had no place at the conference table, disturbing its light mist of permissable nuances and *bon-mots*. Alexander had not changed fundamentally, but the ideals of youth had developed into the ideas of middle age, now more than tinged with an opulent piety. LaHarpe, the third of the trinity of Swiss influences, was ever by his side with ideas as humanistic as those of his compatriots were godly. The platform which condemned Napoleon as an evil genius was one of liberty and enlightenment, notions calculated to strike fear into European allies who had not yet recovered from the shock of the French Revolution despite the extraordinary changes and upheavals which followed it.

It was suspected, once again then as now, that Russia hoped to spread subversion on the continent by mobilizing revolutionary opinion behind her banner, and thereby contribute to the overthrow of European society. The fall of Napoleon left very much the same vacuum as the fall of Hitler was to do a century and a half later, and in the cautious reassessment of the various prevailing influences, Russia caused similar reactions in the camp of the victors.

In both cases, she had survived great patriotic wars and made sacrifices beyond the technical capacities of most other nations, thereby engendering awe but creating new fears. There was less enigma in recent

Napoleon broods over burning Moscow.

George Daw, the portrait painter, visited in his studio at the Winter Palace by Alexander I. The walls of the studio are covered by portraits of Alexander's generals.

history because of the proclaimed dogma of the Soviet state, but in 1814 no one knew for sure to what extent the paradoxical personality of Alexander was really a mouthpiece for the state he ruled, or whether he was just profiting by his prolonged absence from St Petersburg to vent his personal theories which had no chance of ultimate acceptance by the dark powers which loitered in the wings. Whatever the truth, his was a disturbing influence in a conference of professional diplomats unused to the expression of ideals, and therefore mistrustful of their perpetrator.

The English, ever gravitating towards the status quo as a known horror preferable to the unknown horror of social experiment, talked about a just equilibrium in Europe, and the British Foreign Secretary, Viscount Castlereagh, asked Alexander how the continued occupation of Polish soil by the Russians could be reconciled with the woolly ideals of a Holy Alliance of European powers based on a general acceptance of principle.

This was a sly blow below the belt, a gratuitous change of emphasis from the general to the particular calculated to undermine the broad sweep of argument by reverting to the familiar preoccupation with back-biting over details which had the advantage of familiarity to mere negotiations. In fact, a new constitution for Poland went some way to placate the Poles in their heartcries for a national identity. Alexander, though accused of talking 'exalted nonsense' by the least virulent of his detractors, nevertheless stuck to his guns, and declared that free constitutions would be the logical outcome of his doctrines. He saved France from dismemberment at the hands of the victors after the apotheosis of the Napoleonic adventure at Waterloo by insisting on a constitution which would, to use his own words, 'unite the crown and representatives of the people in a sense of common interest'. Continued Swiss independence was assumed, and the stirrings of constitutional freedom in Russia were protected, at least for a time, from the jealousy of Austria.

It was a curious irony that Alexander was able to do for other, smaller nations what he was singularly unable to do at home, and certainly the misgivings of liberal opinion about him was largely due to the fact that while he practised what he preached in a disorganized Europe, he was still the autocratic ruler of a country which lay a few centuries behind Europe in education, organization and general welfare. This looked like hypocrisy, but it was in fact the result of circumstances which were beyond one man's control.

As he grew older, he became more pragmatic without restricting the horizons of his mind. Castlereagh fell out with Metternich, accusing him of inciting governments to contract alliances against the peoples. Alexander agreed with Castlereagh, but as the incidences of revolutionary activity throughout a convalescent Europe increased alarmingly, he formulated more cautious ideas about liberty in general. 'It should be confined within just limits. And the limits of liberty are the principles of order.'

Metternich believed that a collective Europe should reserve for itself the right to interfere in the internal affairs of sovereign states which, in the judgment of the majority, infringed the letter or spirit of the agreement. Alexander held out for a long time against this, but finally became a signatory to this concession in 1820. A grave precedent was set which lowered the sights of the Holy Alliance, and made it once more prey to the most powerful of its signatories.

Once he was back in Russia, the dormant nation covered him like a mantle with the weight of its ancient prejudices. Alexander I died in Taganrog on 1 December 1825, at the age of only forty-seven. As he said himself, he was crushed by the terrible weight of a crown.

In a way, he was the greatest of Russian monarchs, in that he was less suited to the role than many of his predecessors, and yet made supreme efforts to fulfil his destiny, not only as an Emperor but as a man. He never gave up the unequal battle between his private existence and his public image. Married at the age of sixteen to the Princess Maria Louisa of Baden for purely political reasons, his private life was empty, although the death of their only child drew them together, and they ended their lives in a touching harmony. This progression was somehow typical of Alexander.

However melancholy his disposition by the end of his life, however eroded by the wear and tear of endless decisions, there was about him a dogged steadiness of purpose and a basic goodness which outlasted all the transitory tribulations of office. Unlike the great Tsars who had preceded him, he acquired neither the titles of 'Great' nor 'Terrible', but remained merely 'the First', which is itself not merely a numeral but a verity, for he was indeed the first to carry Russia's influence into the world, where it was greeted with misgiving because it was Russian, and also because it took an entirely different form from what had been expected. He was also the first Russian ruler for whom, through the filter of the years, we can feel not only admiration, but even affection, which is perhaps the greatest compliment of all.

The Russia he left was very different to the one he had found, while remaining depressingly the same. The problem never changed: by keeping the windows closed you could regulate the temperature of the room at the risk of stifling the occupants, but by opening the windows, you could no longer control the quantity or quality of the insects which came in as a natural adjunct to fresh air. There was an endless series of attempts to open the window an inch or two, while swatting whatever flew in. At the time of Alexander's death, the window was closed again. The Ministry of Education was linked to the Ministry of Spiritual Affairs in a misguided effort to spread ecumenical fervour throughout the processes of learning. The campaign, which proclaimed religious freedom, with equality of other forms of worship with the Orthodox Church, was placed under the guidance of the chief of the Russian branch of the Bible Society who also happened to be the Procurator of the Holy Synod. Nothing could be more calculated to provoke the opposition of the conservatives in the Orthodox Church, and as a result of their pressure, the high hopes of the reformers were thwarted, and the purpose of their reforms changed. Universities were emasculated, and valuable textbooks confiscated, since no learning of any kind was tolerated which did not have its basis in holy writ. Alexander's appointee was forced subsequently to resign after he had been anathematized by the archimandrite Foti.

As though they recognized that the weight of the crown had indeed become intolerable, neither Alexander's two heirs wished to assume it. Konstantin, his brother, had renounced the throne two years previously, to the evident anguish of Nicholas, the youngest of the three brothers, who swore allegiance to Konstantin in the hope of making him change his mind. When he refused, Nicholas threatened to leave Russia and live as an exile.

It was clear that a close observation of the cares of a Tsar, who was supposed to lead the nation in a direction prescribed by the most reactionary elements in a long tradition of obscurantism was enough to induce a veritable panic in the two brothers.

The Decembrist uprising was quelled in Senate Square outside the Winter Palace after Nicholas I had ordered the troops to fire on the crowds.

Naturally the conservatives were no longer unopposed in this age of convulsion and change. The conspirators were no longer stray Cossacks who profited from the vastness of the territory to raise rebel bands far away from the centres of power. Now they were intellectuals operating in the capital, men who gathered not in distant fields, but in smoke-filled salons, a stone's throw from the palaces and the Ministries.

A group of such men, high-minded, yet impractical, most of them serving officers, tried to organize a palace revolution of the Guards' Regiments in favour of the abdicated Konstantin, and to compel the unwilling Nicholas I, who had by now become Tsar, to adopt a liberal constitution. The uprising, which captured the romantic imagination, was a failure. Indeed it perhaps captured the romantic imagination because it was a failure. Several of the so-called *Dekabristi* (the Decembrists) were executed, while others were banished to Siberia.

A failure it may have been, but from then on Russia was never without her plotters, from visionary aristocratic idealists to murky terrorists arguing endlessly in garrets, while designing infernal machines for the speedy dispatch of high officials. And because of this furtive under-current in the mainstream of life, Russia was never without her secret police either, or without her informers and double-agents. In that respect, she had not only caught up with the practices of Europe, she was actually ahead of them. Nicholas I, the Unwilling, became Tsar at a time least propitious for his personal safety.

War in the Crimea

Nicholas was somewhat taciturn, abrupt in manner, ungainly where Alexander had been graceful, but not of a temperament to wear himself out with introspection. He did not seek to know what to do, but contented himself with finding out how things should be done. Although he sought the advice of some of Alexander's wisest counsellors, he did not act on what they told him, but merely formed a sub-committee to lay out for him all possible areas ripe for reform. Having heard them out, and even gone to the ideas of the *Dekabristi* for inspiration, he slammed the windows shut more securely than ever.

As others before him, he decided that education was the area which required particular attention in a country with Russia's problems of illiteracy. However, his solutions were not quite what people expected. He decided to confine education exclusively to the upper class, that small section of the population which needed it least. To educate the lower orders appeared to him unnecessarily dangerous. Only the off-spring of the gentry and of civil servants could now be admitted to university. Alexander's liberal statutes were rescinded.

It might seem that his decrees would set Russia back for centuries, but he was too late. The effects of Alexander's earlier encouragement of learning now began to develop in surprising ways. The intellectuals in their salons and cafés began discussions of quite a different character, in searching for a true Russian soul impervious to influence, the soul of a pristine people organizing themselves along instinctive lines before the first Tartar had ever appeared in their midst to cloud the issues.

This was in any case the century of soul-searching of independence movements, and of intense nationalism. Before the century's end the German Chancellor, Bismarck, would have united Germany and Cavour and Garibaldi would have done the same for Italy. There was revolt and upheaval in the air, and Russia was no exception, except for the fact that she was not trying to shake herself free from oppression imposed from outside, but oppression imposed from within.

Some socialist thinkers believed that Russian instincts were collective by nature, as witness the ancient social structure of the tribal village, and that therefore they were the only truly instinctive socialist or communist people, interesting in the light of future developments. To this they added a patriotic rider which suggested that a collective soul was superior to an individual one, and that Russia had some sort of divine mission towards the rest of the world, still labouring under the illusion of the importance of the individual mind, the individual conscience.

These Slavophiles included Dostoevsky in his early days which did not prevent him from being arrested and led out to be executed for the

Nicholas I (1796–1855).

Nicholas, the Empress Alexandra and the future Alexander II on their yacht.

crime of reading banned literature. At the last moment, he was reprieved by a galloping horseman bearing a pardon, which commuted his sentence to some years in Siberia, a nasty joke by the authorities which Dostoevsky paid back by writing banned literature which has survived its epoch and all its holy cows.

The Pan-Slav movement had something of the Gothic revival about it, a search for archaic roots at the expense of all that had developed since. All contact with the West was reviled as having caused a plague of false values which sullied the romanticized innocence of the noble savages who had first called themselves Russian. The image of the past was simplified to the point of being a stained-glass window set before a blinding sun. Peter the Great was a fool who had looked far and wide for that which lay at his very feet and in the radiant sky above him.

There were, of course, other intellectuals in other salons and in other coffee-houses, eventually in London or Zurich or Paris, who believed just the opposite, without for a moment negating the search for roots which was the hallmark of their times. Alexander Herzen published his influential magazine, *Kolokol*, (the Bell), in exile, and the powerful socialist theorist Mikhail Bakunin also emigrated abroad, which was understandable since they both believed in the Western origin of Russian culture, and that everything which could be done to occidentalize it, should be done.

Meanwhile Nicholas was suffering from his own delusions. Whereas Alexander had seen the work of God spread with evangelic generosity among all peoples of goodwill, Nicholas now claimed God for himself, and a divine mission for his armies.

His ludicrous declaration of 1848, 'Submit yourselves, ye people, for God is with us,' was only one of many such pieces of blasphemous bombast uttered by rulers, culminating in the Kaiser's notorious '*Gott Mit Uns!*' as a foretaste of carnage in the First World War. The trouble with such *dicta* is that the perpetrators begin to believe their own utterances, and it is remarkable with what alacrity God deserts them.

It had already been established by treaty during the reign of Catherine that Russia was the protector of the Christian minorities within the Ottoman Empire, and Nicholas thought that this gave him the right to allocate the places of worship in Jerusalem to the Orthodox clergy at the expense of Catholics and the many other denominations who worshipped there. He issued an ultimatum to Turkey, which was rejected. He then attacked the Turks, and his fleet scattered a Turkish squadron in the Black Sea.

The British saw in this a sinister design on the trade route to India, while France was eager for revenge for the humiliating occupation of Paris by Russian troops, among others, in 1815. These two powers were thus allied for the first time in two hundred years. They were joined by Austria, who regarded Russian expansionism with alarm, despite the fact that the Emperor of that country owed his throne to Russian military intervention on his behalf only five years previously.

At the very beginning of 1854, the British officer in charge of preparation for war, Sir John Burgoyne, an engineer, concurred with the French Minister of War, another engineer, that defence was the best method of attack, and with Turkish agreement, they erected powerful defences at Gallipoli. The trouble was that the Russians were not prepared to attack. An allied expeditionary force was assembled at Varna, in Bulgaria. There the Russians delivered another underhand blow by responding to an Austrian ultimatum by withdrawing their troops from the area south of the Danube. There was now no cause for war. However, this detail failed to upset the new alliance, especially since an epidemic of typhus had broken out among the waiting troops. It was decided that advance was more honourable than retreat, and the Crimean War broke out on schedule.

There can never have been a war in the whole history of conflict so ill-prepared for by all parties, and so stupidly conducted. The British Admiralty possessed a map of the Crimea, but no indication that the

Balaklava harbour and encampment.
A photograph taken in 1853.

depth of the water around the isthmus was nowhere deep enough to lap higher than a man's waist, a fact it was to find out on the spot. Napoleon III appears not even to have had a reliable map, but a couple of water-colours by the academician Raffet provided invaluable information about the general appearance of Sebastopol and Balaklava. These paintings were removed from the wall of the Salon, and studied assiduously by strategists.

The warship *Caradoc*, with the British commander and his staff on board, sailed in advance of the main fleet in order to select a suitable landing place. They observed Russian officers on shore watching them through telescopes, and when it became apparent that both sides could see each other, hats were doffed in formal greeting. Eupatoria was selected by general consensus as an ideal landing place, and an ultimatum was sent ashore. The Governor fumigated the document before studying it and invited the Allied Advance Guard ashore, but warning

A Russian army encampment in the Crimea.

them that while on Russian soil, they must consider themselves in quarantine.

This tone of farce was present relentlessly throughout the miseries of this war, which lasted two full years, costing many lives to disease as well as to fighting. Florence Nightingale moved through the ranks of the dying with her lamp held high, drawing attention to the scandalously low standards of sanitation, while perhaps even more influential, the war correspondent of *The Times*, William Russell, wrote objective reports so much to the point that he was referred to as 'low and grovelling' by military mouths under their crisp moustaches.

To add to the feeling of hopeless, inextricable muddle, Lord Raglan, the British Commander-in-Chief, who had last seen service at Waterloo almost half a century before, never could bring himself to refer to the enemy as anything but 'The French'.

It is safe to say that despite the many heroic actions and brilliant local feats of arms such as the ridiculous but glorious Charge of the Light Brigade, the incredible chapter of accidents perpetrated by the coalition was only successful because the Russians were just that little bit worse.

Nicholas died, broken by the failure of his pretensions and the gods' disloyal defection, on 22 March 1855.

Shooting the Rapids

Alexander II, who succeeded his father, was a thin, stylish man without a strong personality, but affable in manner. During his father's strict reign, there had been as many as 556 separate peasant uprisings of no national consequence, but their number, and the consistency with which they took place, made it clear that the general unrest could no longer be ignored, especially in the light of the disgrace of the Crimean War, which made it obvious that not only was Russian military equipment obsolete but more important that the bureaucratic structure was cumbersome and inefficient when dealing with realities of any kind.

It was suddenly clear, not merely to agitators, that the system of serfdom was archaic. That it was inhuman did not matter as much to the establishment as the fact that it no longer served its historical purpose. Instead of unquestioning order, it now bred discontent, and seemed to educated opinion barbarous and a living proof to the rest of the world that Russia was irrevocably behind the times.

Alexander was not insensitive to the speed of the current which was carrying him inexorably towards certain vital yet epoch-making decisions. He faced them courageously as he declared to an assembly of the nobles in Moscow that the situation was untenable. 'It is better', he declared, 'to abolish serfdom from above than to wait for it to be abolished from below.'

The nobles considered that their traditional privileges were being menaced, and did everything they could to slow the approach of the inevitable day. The situation was a recurring one but as time passed the serfs became more vociferous, the nobles more uncompromising, and the secret police had to work overtime unearthing nihilist plots. This anarchist sect was not unlike the mindless terrorists of the late-twentieth century. Their avowed aim was to destroy society utterly, so that it would be forced back into a second springtime. Society is too large a target for groups of desperate men with a bomb or two at their disposal, but they can certainly do a lot of damage on their way to their undoing.

The proposals and counterproposals for effecting serf emancipation dragged on for nearly two years, with forty-six provincial committees all contributing. The nobles managed to reduce the sizes of the land reserved for emancipated serfs, and increase their rents, but despite the opposition of much of the nobility, the law was passed on 9 Feburary 1861. On 10 February, far away in another, newer country divided on basically the same issue, Abraham Lincoln was installed as President of the United States.

The landowners in Russia tried their utmost to retain their predominance in local affairs, but the freed peasants outwitted them by

A religious procession in the Russia of Alexander II, painted by Ilya Repin.

organizing village communes, with elected elders in charge. The collectives spoke against the individual.

Within three years an entire reorganization of local government came into force in which landowners held 48 per cent of the seats, the inhabitants of urban communities 12 per cent, and the peasants 40 per cent. Despite the imbalance which this distribution of influence displayed, it marked an amazing leap forward. Roads improved, as did medical services. There was free distribution of medicine for the needy. Schools had fewer students per class. Hospitals increased almost fourfold, the number of doctors doubled as did their salaries.

The same year, the legal system was completely overhauled. There were independent courts with permanent judges. There was trial by jury and professional lawyers pleaded in public.

Naturally no reform is ever so far-reaching as to please the extremists, for whom any concession seems like a weakening of authority, any gesture of goodwill read as fear. In 1866, a student by name Dmitri Karakozov, shot at the Tsar as he was climbing into his carriage, and missed.

Authority does not like its motives to be misunderstood, and so that there should be no doubts, repressive measures become the order of the day. Diehard right wingers took over from liberals, and still the attempts at regicide went on, while endless revolutionary movements replaced or

Tsar Alexander II during the Balkan
Campaign in 1878.

duplicated each other, with names as evocative of idealism and menace
as 'Land and Liberty', 'Black Partition', and 'The Will of the People'.
In 1879, a man called Solovyov fired five shots at the Tsar. They all
missed. The next year, a young labourer, Khalturin, blew up the court
diningroom at the Winter Palace, but it was between meals. A special
commission was formed under the direction of a General Loris-Melikov
to try and enlist public support in the fight against terrorism. He came
up with a plan which promised a further great increase in private liberties on the condition that terrorism was completely eradicated. He
attempted to mobilize the nation in its vigilance of any suspicious
occurrences with the promise of liberalization as a reward for its
patriotism and devotion to the Crown. The same day as Alexander II
signed the decree he was the subject of yet another attempt on his life
when a small bomb fell near his carriage as he returned home from
dinner with his aunt. Some of the Cossacks of his bodyguard were
wounded. He alighted from his carriage to help them, and mildly chided
the man who had thrown the bomb. Then he paused to thank the
Almighty for his deliverance. 'It is too early to thank God,' shouted a
young man in the crowd, as he threw a second bomb. 'Take me home to
die,' murmured the Tsar, his shattered body streaming with blood.

It is hard to know just how many of the extraordinary developments
of Alexander II's reign were his responsibility. We are tempted to think,
not very many of them. He just happened to be at the helm when the
ship of state shot the rapids. Russia was a burgeoning country, in the
grip of an industrial revolution. One expression of this economic
development was the number of private banks founded at this time. 10
Agricultural Credit Banks opened during his reign, together with 28

commercial banks, 71 Mutual Credit Organizations and no less than 222 municipal banks.

While Europe was in the grip of the usual minuet of changing partners, the Russia of Alexander expanded greatly in Asia. Bokhara was taken and the shores of the Caspian assured. The frontiers of Afghanistan were reached, and she nibbled at China. The port of Vladivostok was founded, and the peninsula of Sakhalin was exchanged with Japan against two of the Kurile Islands.

As had been said before, the landlocked traditions of Russia, despite her relatively recent access to various seas, dictated a form of expansionism quite different from that of the colonial powers. Her few overseas adventures only confirmed her in her predilection for solid lines of communication to her home base. She had, of course, ventured overseas to Alaska, which she colonized half-heartedly for the animal pelts, and extended her tentacles as far down the Californian Coast as Fort Ross, but all her penetrations had something wary and impermanent about them. She even, for a while, occupied one of the Hawaiian Islands, but there was nothing more liable to underscore a Russian's nostalgia for his own Northern discomfort than bare-breasted women crooning in grass skirts. The end of the Russian overseas adventure came in 1867, when she sold Alaska to the Americans for just $7,200,000. 'Seward's Folly' was one of the best deals the United States ever made. It should have been called 'Alexander's Folly'.

The Open Window

From now until the great revolution which was to destroy the grudgingly changing fabric of Russian institutions thirty-six years later, there was no let up in intellectual or terrorist pressures on the government. There had already been a gigantic breakthrough in public relations, if one can apply to the arts this somewhat pejorative and diminishing description. It was through the arts that western observers formed their image of the new Russia. It is true that the impact of Pushkin's poetry was far greater on Russians than on foreigners, owing to the difficulties of translating adequately his subtle style, with its relentless metre and its declamatory irony. Both Alexander Pushkin (1799–1837) and his brilliant young contemporary Mikhail Lermontov (1814–1841) were killed in stupid duels, which reached epidemic proportions as a result of the spread of this peculiarly Western pastime among the romantic, fatalistic youth of St Petersburg. Pushkin was thirty-eight at the time of his death; Lermontov only twenty-seven.

Prose stood a better chance of spreading the gospel of the Russian literary genius. Nikolai Gogol (1809–1852) liberated his writing from the classical division of the comic and the tragic into separate artistic compartments and became the first great Russian realist. Russian literature, developing late, shook itself free of the shackles of courtly refinements and concentrated on realistic observation of life. Life, the new Russian writers seemed to say, is a rich mixture of the tragic and the comic, the unpredictable and the undefinable, and its only consistent quality is its inconsistency. Gogol was, at heart, a thorough-going romantic as befits the period in which he worked, but his corrosive pen, and his savage satirical sense gives his work a grotesque quality which is profoundly Russian.

It is impossible to be more than insultingly superficial in such a brief assessment of the rise of Russian literature, but the idea is not to do justice to this weighty subject in the available space, but merely to assess the effect which its spread had on the outside observer. Here was a light shed on the way life was lived in Russia and, revealed too, was the surprising genius which at least a handful of 'baptized bears' possessed in plumbing the depths of human motivation, desire, and inconsistency.

Gogol's sparkling comedy, *The Inspector General*, and his great novel, *Dead Souls*, gave a new dimension to the Russian's realization of his own human and bureaucratic shortcomings by means of a weapon which had been missing from the national armoury, laughter. In his comedy, *Marriage*, he moreover created a character, later amplified by Goncharov in his superb *Oblomov*, of the Russian incapable of making

Alexander Pushkin (1799–1837), painted in 1835, two years before his death.

up his mind about anything, who takes refuge in his own sloth, and whose relief from pressing problems like rising from bed is a catnap. This figure was instantly recognized as being typical, and a word, the equivalent of 'Oblomovism', passed rapidly into general usage to describe that particular indolence brought about by distance, monotony, and the kind of simple comfort a dog finds before a fire.

Somewhere there is a description of the Scythians as becoming extinct through an 'excess of humour'. A virile nomadic race settled down among pleasant surroundings, and gradually became totally immobile, both in fact and in spirit. There was no point going to the next room. You already knew what was there. There was finally no point in anything, since adventure was tiring, sport was transitory, its benefits wearing off in next to no time, and imagination could do the work of mere energy much more effectively.

edor Dostoevsky (1821–81), painted
y Vassily Perov in 1872.

The malaise was not confined to the nobility. Although serfs had done the manual work, they shared with their owners a peculiar torpor, the lullaby of horizons without end, the feeling of existing unobserved in a backwater where time had no great meaning since every passing minute bore a striking similarity to the one which had preceded it.

In the middle of the nineteenth century Russian letters reached their full flowering. Three figures above all dominated their times, and showed not only that the nation had come of age, but that in some respects they led their contemporaries in other lands in the objectivity of their writing, their unflinching stare at the nakedness of man in even the politest of societies.

Ivan Turgenev (1818–1883) was the oldest of the three, a man of a melancholy aristocracy, savaged in his childhood by a terrible mother, and creator, in his wan tales of the provinces, of a gallery of powerful women and indeterminate men. He spent a great deal of his time outside Russia, and by that fact alone, became more Russian than ever. His works are not generally considered to be quite in the class of his greatest contemporaries, but that is the stuff of critics. He remains in some important respects, by virtue of his reticence and impeccable taste, his unwillingness to force himself upon the reader, and his nostalgic evocation of dangerous moods like boredom, the most national of Russian authors.

Fedor Dostoevsky (1821–1881) was a writer of undoubted greatness, whose ferocious probing into human motivation, conscious and unconscious, set new standards in understanding and compassion. His great novels such as *Crime and Punishment* and *The Brothers Karamazov* are works of immense power and unrelieved tension, and have about them a febrile compulsion, as though they had to be written despite the pain and anguish their writing occasioned.

Photograph of Nikolai Rimsky-
rsakov (1844–1908).

If Turgenev was the kindly and ineffectual family doctor of the trio, and Dostoevsky was the surgeon, Leo Tolstoy (1828–1910) was the faith healer. A huge shaggy man who had spent a dissolute youth, he turned to writing and quickly made it a profession rather than an amusing hobby for a Count. His manner was more measured than Dostoevsky's, who used to dictate rather than write, and who was an epileptic. Tolstoy's style was more rational, more detached, less frantically involved with the action, but this cooler perception only added to his convincing portrait of a most feminine woman in Anna Karenina, and his intensely personal reconstruction of an entire era, peopled with extraordinarily interesting characters, in *War and Peace*.

As he grew older, a certain patriarchal mysticism gripped him. He began to cobble with village shoemakers, wrote diatribes against tobacco, and conveniently came to consider sex immoral when he reached his eighties. He ended his life as a kind of rural King Lear, in the company of his beloved youngest daughter. He breathed his last in a

The cast from an 1891 production of
The Sleeping Beauty

country railway station at the age of eighty-two while trying to escape from oppressive domesticity.

Music, being abstract by nature, had less of an impact on the West's image of Russia. For years she had imported Italian directors for her opera, and homegrown products were regarded with some misgivings, and even scoffed at as being Russian, and for that reason, inept.

There were one or two early exceptions to this rule, notably Dmitri Bortnyansky (1751–1825), an illegitimate son of a nobleman and a serf woman. He showed such talent that he was sent to Italy and came back with some astonishingly individual operas, notably *The Falcon*, in a distinctly Mozartian style, but predating Mozart's great operas by several years.

Later he turned exclusively to music for the Orthodox Church, much of it of quite unusual beauty.

Mikhail Glinka (1804–1857) is considered the first real fully-fledged Russian composer, although distinctly Italianate in his operas despite their native themes. Tchaikovsky (1840–1893) was considered to be Western by Russian nationalists, despite the Russian titles of his early symphonies, but in him the country acquired its first musician of international consequence. His highly charged emotional temperament was controlled by a more than competent musical technique.

Although the descriptive powers of a great novelist make an immediate impact on the reader, music is perhaps even more illustrative of the extremes of the Russian temperament. The strong academic tradition in Russian music prescribed obedience to rigid rules which had developed by cautious evolution over the centuries. These rules had to be mastered by the student, even if it entailed years of laborious and joyless application, whatever the musician's natural bent. Alexander Taneiev (1850–1918) was an example of the Russian pedagogue, who often has the capacity of making his German counterparts seem like veritable ballerinas of the classroom. Both Taneiev and Rimsky-Korsakov (1844–1908) wrote endless fugues in order to master the art, and Balakirev (1837–1910), although an emancipator, eager to promote musical nationalism, became very quickly an intolerable martinet. He imposed strict rules where a modicum of fresh air should have flowed and became so finicky that he objected to musicians marrying, on the crabbed assumption that a true musician could not serve two masters.

Mili Balakirev (1837–1910), a drawing by Leon Bakst.

LEFT: Modest Mussorgsky (1835–81) by Ilya Repin.

It is conceivable that this trend was a direct result of that painful process of 'catching up with the West' instituted by Peter the Great. The rigid academic philosophy of the Russian musical establishment was first cousin to the bellowing of German drill masters, imported to instil in Russian recruits the terrors of the parade ground, with its nonsensical orders and disproportionate punishment for real or imagined offences, such as cleaning paving stones with a toothbrush.

RIGHT: The great Russian bass, Chaliapin, in the title role of *Boris Godunov*.

Writing fugues for the sake of writing fugues is not unlike cleaning paving stones with a toothbrush.

At the other end of the spectrum was that isolated genius Mussorgsky (1839–1881), self-taught and self-teaching, who was guided by his instinct and ability to improvise at the piano. Deeply and genuinely admired by his colleagues for the utter independence of his mind, they were nevertheless unsparing with their advice on how to improve his works; in other words, how to make them more acceptable to critical opinion, and more dramatically effective to the conventional operatic ear. He did make things difficult for the good musical samaritans around him by spending practically his entire career in making false starts; a fragment of *Han d'Islande* followed by a fragment of *Salammbo*, in its turn followed by an unfinished *Mlada*, an incomplete *Sorochinsky Fair*, and at last, apart from some superb songs and a few piano pieces, the great masterpiece *Boris Godunov*, avidly reorchestrated by Rimsky-Korsakov, and later, as a commission, by Shostakovich. With the passage of time, the full modernity of the original is becoming apparent. Mussorgsky was truly Russia making his solitary way through the jungle of possible sounds without help or influence, except that of his inherited languages, words and song.

He captured as no one before or since the power and solace of the musical phrase based on spoken thought-phrases, against a jagged, splintered musical background. Words are spoken, sobbed out, choked, as the Tsar dies, while the distant chorus ploughs its archaic furrows of sound in the dark, dank air. The terrors and beauty of the occasion are expressed by means as unusual as they are personal, owing nothing to cumulative noise or orchestral splendours, owing everything to sudden, unpredictable changes of direction, as in the madrigals of Monteverdi or the greatest of Shakespeare's speeches. He turned his own short-windedness, his lack of professional stamina, to his advantage in this masterpiece, which not even the love and admiration of his friends could destroy, and which stands as an unequalled comment on Russia at a certain vulnerable period in her epos.

Of the others, Borodin, Rimsky-Korsakov and Balakirev, Borodin (1833–1887) was probably the most individual, and remarkable for being a celebrated chemist, one of whose papers is still referred to. But the passing of years has seen the Westerner Tchaikovsky accepted as the most Russian of all, with the evident exception of Mussorgsky.

This totally inadequate catalogue is merely to show that there were voices which spoke for Russia in the comity of civilized people other than those of ministers and Tsars, and those of their assailants.

In fact, the personality of rulers was becoming less and less important now that the *dramatis personae* of the nation included practically its entire population. Special conditions may have been peculiar to Russia, but the circumstances were duplicated in practically every

ABOVE: Charge of the Heavy Brigade at Balaklava on 25 October 1854. Russian troops were routed on the banks of the Alma.
BELOW: A contemporary cartoon showing the alliance between Russia and Turkey during the Crimean War.

AN ALLEGORY

developed nation. The conspiracy of classes had become worldwide, and it has never respected frontiers since.

The activities of the terrorists diminished slightly with the accession of Alexander III, not because the perpetrators held out any hopes for change, but because they were exhausted. As a consequence the authorities were able, for a while, to diminish the carrot once again, while increasing the size of the stick. It is one of the strange characteristics of intransigence that it increases in obtuseness when its days are numbered.

There were concessions, but on the whole life for the ordinary Russian was ever more strictly regulated. A peasants' bank was opened, but also a nobles' bank, with the avowed aim of helping to preserve the lands of the gentry from expropriations due to debt. Whereas increased industrialization brought benefits, it also brought certain perplexities. There was a gigantic increase in foreign investment, but a commensurate leap in protectionist tariffs on foreign goods, which moved from 13 per cent to 37 per cent. At the same time, the price of grain, the staple export of Russia then, dropped by over a half. The first famine of 1891 did nothing to relieve the financial problems of the authorities.

With all these libertarian crosscurrents, there were still those who insisted on the virtues of autocratic rule. Pobedonostsev, the Prime Minister, even formulated a motive for his activities which was the height of avuncular cynicism. He spoke of 'prolonging Russia's youth'. It was, of course, far too late for that. All he succeeded in doing for a short time, which was much more risky, was to prolong Russia's adolescence. He began a whole series of religious persecutions which were not, contrary to general belief, exclusively aimed at the Jews, but which included Lutherans, members of Uniate sects, Kalmyks, and others who did not conform to the 'true beliefs' of the majority of the population.

Foreign affairs during this period of oppression were fairly calm, owing to Alexander III's accommodation with Bismarck and the now united Germany. Despite his initial *entente* with Austro-Hungary, which was avowedly anti-Russian in character, Bismarck extended a hand to Russia which was gratefully accepted as a guarantee against England, Russia's principal rival in Asia. Later, when Bismarck continued his setting of the stage for the First World War, which was to break out in just over thirty years' time, by including Italy in the triple alliance, Russia grew suspicious of his motives, and extended an offer of reconciliation to France. The *Entente Cordiale*, which later included Britain, was signed in 1894, and all the pawns, bishops and kings were in place for the hideous massacre which was to follow twenty years later with the outbreak of world war.

Alexander died the same year, an autocrat to the end, but one who lived his life in mortal fear of sudden death.

The coronation of Alexander II in the Kremlin in 1856

CHAPTER ELEVEN

The Seeds of Revolution

Nicholas II was another of the many Tsars who would rather not have reigned. He was perhaps even more addicted to the dream of the quiet life than any other ruler, and yet, like La Fontaine's frog, he had to blow himself up to unnatural proportions in order to assume the unforgiving dimension of autocracy.

With the ubiquitous Pobedonostsev breathing over his shoulder he announced, in reply to the hopes of well-wishers at his marriage, that he was fully aware that senseless dreams had been entertained by certain people to the effect that members of local *zemstvos* might soon enjoy a voice in the internal government of the country. 'Let all know that I intend to uphold the principles of autocracy as unswervingly as did my father.'

Perhaps sensing that this magniloquence came from a man incapable of upholding so much as a personal opinion, the progressive elements retorted sharply and with unaccustomed unanimity. Particularly stung by the new Tsar's reference to dreams about a popular participation in government being senseless, they warned him not to be prey to senseless dreams about his own powers. They warned that autocracy was digging its own grave if it considered the dictates of its own bureaucracy to be omnipotent. If it wished for a struggle, it only had to continue along its chosen path.

The reply was as peremptory, and as full of dire promise as the Tsar's declaration had been.

Two years later, St Petersburg experienced its first strike, in which as many as thirty thousand workmen participated. Marxist socialism showed its hand for the first time.

Student riots spread over the south of Russia. The Minister of Public Education, Bogolyepov, threatened the ringleaders with compulsory military service. The reply was even harsher than that of the progressives to the Tsar. Bogolyepov was killed by a student. Two months later, the Minister of the Interior, Sipyagin was assassinated in his turn. Those accused of political crimes increased five fold in nine years.

It is not unusual for reactionary governments under internal pressure to seek relief from their problems by launching foreign adventures designed to awaken patriotic sentiments. The Trans-Siberian Railway had been completed, and William II of Germany expressed the belief, comforting for himself, that Russia's destiny lay not in the West, but in the East.

Russia foolishly took the hint, finding in this cunning suggestion the very relief she was looking for. The Russian East Asiatic Industrial Company was a speculative commercial enterprise in which many

In January 1905 Father Gapon led a delegation of workers to the Winter Palace to confront the Tsar.

influential capitalists, including the Tsar himself, held shares. In its name, the Russians began an expansion in Manchuria which provoked a protest from Japan, an unknown quantity believed by the Russians to be backward and ignorant of the techniques of modern warfare. Japan concluded a treaty with England, and so the disgruntled Russians promised to remove their troops from Manchuria by a certain date. This they failed to do. On 5 February 1904 the Japanese surprised the world, including of course, Russia, by destroying a large part of the Russian Pacific fleet, at anchor in the harbour of Port Arthur. The Russians, insulted, immediately instituted a punitive expedition by land and sea.

The army was transported by the Trans-Siberian Railway, which was, however, a tenuous and restricted lifeline. The army's equipment was adequate, but none too modern. General Dragomirov, the Minister of War, one of the long series of bewhiskered military duffers produced by all countries in extraordinary profusion between 1850 and 1918, declined the introduction of field telephones into his army with the memorable phrase, 'There is nothing which can be said by telephone which cannot be said more effectively by man to man.'

The war by land was largely inconclusive owing to the vast area of hostilities. Divisions and army corps frequently retired after apparent local successes for fear of being cut off, so infinite were the flanks and

Russian troops in Manchuria during
the Russo-Japanese war of 1905.

hinterland. The same cannot be said for the war at sea. Russia, deprived
of her most brilliant Admiral, Makarov, whose ship had been blown up
by a mine, now sent her Baltic fleet half way round the world to punish
the Japanese. Its progress round Africa, across the Indian Ocean and
the China Seas was a fascinating odyssey in itself. Near the Dogger Bank,
off the English coast, the Russians opened fire on a group of British
trawlers, killing some fishermen. They were no doubt very trigger
happy, but it really stretches the imagination to believe that, despite a
hazy conception of geography, they took the British to be enterprising
Japanese. The tension which followed between Britain and Russia was
symbolized by a British squadron which followed the Russians for a
considerable period. In Madagascar, the Russian Admiral Rozhdestvensky heard about the defeat of his colleague, Prince Ukhtomsky, and

the Japanese occupation of the base of Port Arthur. He thought of turning back, but was reassured by the dispatch of a second fleet under Admiral Negobatov, which joined him in Kanzank Bay, in present day Kampuchea. Rozhdestvensky was a solitary spirit, much addicted to reading in his cabin, who seemed in the grip of a mournful fatalism. From Kamank, the fleet seemed for a while to disappear into the vastness of the Pacific, and the Japanese Admiral Togo wisely chose to wait for it until it was close to its obvious destination.

On 27 May 1905, over seven months after setting sail, the forest of tall funnels appeared on the skyline in the Tsushima Strait. Togo's ships were both faster and more adaptable, and by nightfall the entire Russian fleet had been sunk or crippled. The President of the United States offered his mediation to help to end the conflict, and a degrading peace treaty was signed in Portsmouth, New Hampshire on 23 August, by which Russia evacuated Manchuria, ceded half of the Sakhalin peninsula, surrendered her lease of Kwantung, including Port Arthur, and recognized Korea as a Japanese zone of influence. So much for the patriotic diversions to take the mind of Russians away from the joys of autocracy.

The revolution did not wait for final defeat. Before the Baltic fleet had even set sail, Plehve, the new Minister of the Interior, successor to the assassinated Sipyagin, was blown sky high in his carriage. A crowd of revolutionaries, led by the peculiar Father Gapon, a police informer, revolutionary and religious zealot all in one, marched to the Winter

The Treaty of Portsmouth, New Hampshire, 29 August 1905, which marked the end of the hostilities in the Russo-Japanese war.

A still from a film made at the time which shows the Tsarist troops about to fire on the crowd outside the Winter Palace, St Petersburg, 1905.

Palace, carrying ikons and religious symbols, eager to speak with the little father of all the Russias. The Tsar was away, the Cossacks were not. The troops fired on the crowd, killing no less than a thousand people. In retaliation for this odious act, the Grand Duke Sergei was assassinated in the Kremlin by a social revolutionary activist, Kaliayev. The milder wing of the progressive movement tried again. They sent the Tsar a deputation which repeated their demands for urgent constitutional reforms. They were told that the Tsar's will (what there was of it) was unshakable.

Three months later, however, Nicholas, or rather his advisers, made a gesture towards reform by instituting a Duma or Imperial Parliament. It was, however, to have only consultative, not legislative power, and was entitled merely to prepare laws for an appointed Council of State to accept or reject, more probably the latter. This emasculated assembly was to represent landed gentry to the tune of 34 per cent, burgesses, 23 per cent, and peasants 43 per cent. It will be seen that the peasants had been allowed to increase their representation, but only in a Council which had no powers whatsoever. Nicholas confessed to a delegation of anxious noblemen that he had no intention of abandoning the traditions of the past. Russia's youth was to be prolonged well into middleage.

His apparent stubbornness led to endless and disruptive industrial action, culminating in a general strike which paralysed the nation for five days in October. It affected transport, posts and communications, factories, shops and even schools. Soviets were formed for the first time. The turmoil seemed virtually out of control, and Nicholas, despite the intractable words penned in his name, entertained ideas of abdication.

Count Witte, who had signed the peace with Japan, which was less destructive of national dignity than many had feared, now took over the reins of government, and tried to steer a difficult if not impossible course between extremes of opinion: the Marxist workers and Social Revolutionaries, with their addiction to terrorism on one hand, and the ostrich-like aristocracy, who did not understand why the troubles of large industrial centres should affect the relative peace of their estates, on the other. To add to his other problems, Witte found that, understandably, liberal opinion was extremely sceptical about his ability to reconcile the opposing elements.

In fact, he fought a losing battle, despite his high hopes. On 3 December, the entire Soviet, including Trotsky, its Vice-Chairman in Lenin's absence abroad, was arrested. Despite sporadic street fighting, the army was called out to crush the revolutionary movement, which it did with consummate ruthlessness and violence. The Tsar, encouraged by this, no longer thought of abdicating, but on the contrary came out with the splendidly Utopian promise that the sun of the truth was soon to shine over the length and breadth of the Russian land. He added to this the rider that his autocratic will remained inflexible.

The Duma in session

Troops on the streets of Moscow during the revolution of 1906.

The first Russian elections took place under these circumstances, and resulted in a victory for the Constitutional Democratic Party, the so-called Cadets, and of peasants desiring agricultural reforms. The Socialists boycotted the elections with a very clear premonition of this first Duma's fate.

The initial act of this decapitated form of parliamentary government was to try to pass its own ambitions into law. The plan was ruled inadmissible by the Tsar's Prime Minister. The Duma passed a vote of censure on the Prime Minister but this was ignored by the Council of State.

The Duma went on arguing for a while as though their assembly made some vague sense, but when they arrived for their daily dose of hot air on the morning of 9 January 1906, they found their Parliament house, the Tauride Palace, surrounded by troops, including artillery. It was a hint that the Duma had been dissolved, and that Russia's first flirtation with popular suffrage had ended in failure.

Many of the deputies fled to Viborg, in Finland, from where they appealed to the public for passive resistance in case another Duma should be convoked, reminding the people that they had been elected, and were still their legitimate representatives, even if temporarily deprived of a forum. Stolypin, the new Prime Minister, who had been instrumental in dissolving the first Duma, now attempted to walk the same tightrope from which both Witte and his successor, Goremykin had fallen. The trick was evidently to seem to be introducing reforms without really doing so. His first agrarian reform was cast in this ingenious mould. He tried to give land expropriated from poor peasants to rich peasants, without touching that belonging to the landowning class. Meanwhile he instituted drumhead courts martial for the rapid disposal of all remaining revolutionaries. Pogroms against Jews was another result of the sunlight so relentlessly shed on Nicholas's Russia by a smiling deity.

In March 1907, the second Duma took its place in the Tauride Palace. This time, the Socialists took part, and the vote-counting registered a considerable swing to the left. The peasants captured 97 seats, the Socialists 83, and the Cadets 123 (compared to 187 in the first Duma). Of the remaining seats 36 went to landed gentry and 63 to blind supporters of the Divine Rights of Tsars.

This Duma lasted under two months, and was no more successful than the first, simply because its powers were so limited. The speeches of the Social Democrats were deemed subversive, and their unwillingness to condemn terrorism without qualification was simply scandalous.

The third Duma came into being late the same year, and lasted almost five years by some miracle. The elections for it were only free by Russian standards, although there had been electoral reforms. The Social Democrats had only 14 seats in the new house, and the peasants 14 too, a suspicious drop from 83 and 97 respectively. The Cadets, who now appeared on the left of centre for the first time, were accorded 53, another suspicious fall from 123. So-called Progressives held 39, and Poles and Muslims shared 26 regional seats. In the centre, which was quite far to the right on the Imperial scale, no less than 133 went to the representatives of landed gentry as opposed to 36 earlier in the year, while those who believed the Tsar could do no wrong improved their position from 63 to 145!

At last Russia had a national assembly worthy of a feeble autocrat and the Imperial puppeteers. Poland and Finland were deprived of the last vestiges of autonomy under new legislation, while active measures were undertaken against the Ukrainian separatists and Jews. The convolutions of internal politics were such, and the manoeuvrings to give a democratic appearance to even the most retrogressive legislation were so blatant that nobody really knew where they stood. They merely knew where they had been told to stand. In the midst of this Machiavellian tangle, Stolypin was murdered by a revolutionary and the rumour was that the assassin had acted on the instructions of the police. The worst of it is that, under such circumstances, rumour is often correct.

Stolypin, who was assassinated in 1911

The fourth Duma came into being in 1912, and was no more representative of popular will than the third had been. Admittedly the Progressive vote increased by 9 votes to 48, but the peasants dropped 5 votes, and now only had 9. Meanwhile in the Court, it had been established that the young Tsarevich Alexis was a haemophiliac, the victim of a dreaded disease contracted from his mother's side. Once his blood began to flow it would not clot and death would result from even a superficial scratch. Since he was the only heir to the throne, he was protected from any kind of injury much as the Sleeping Beauty is

Gregory Rasputin

A tea party given for Rasputin by his admirers.

shielded from a pinprick in the Ballet. Every kind of cure was tried. Finally the Tsarina placed her faith in Rasputin, a huge, unkempt but hypnotic holy man out of Russia's mediaeval past. He had a mysterious and emollient effect on the highly strung child. This ingratiated him with the Court, in which he rampaged with the uninhibited power of a bull in a field of cows, extending his influence, through the acquiescence of the superstitious and foolish Tsarina Alexandra, into the world of politics.

This small and increasingly absurd world of a spineless autocrat, his emotional wife, his sick child, and a mad monk lording it over an alleged parliament of hamstrung deputies was saved from utter discredit not only by the bayonets of the soldiery and the whips of the Cossacks, but by the outbreak of the First World War.

War and Revolution

The nations had been spoiling for a general confrontation in Europe even without knowing it. It was not merely that Europe was almost equally divided into two potentially hostile blocs, with every powerful nation engaged, but the moral climate was as highly charged as an overripe fruit ready to fall from the tree. The folly of Empire had reached its apogee, with every monarch wearing the uniform of the other while on state visits, giving each other elaborate Christmas presents, their families indulging in charades and amateur theatricals to while away the intense boredom of Court life. Beneath this rarefied strata big business had become organized and international. There was new wealth to match the old, and new poverty to match the even older.

Russia was merely the extreme case of a malady which was practically universal. Factories in which men, women and children often worked under shocking conditions brought large profits to shareholders while the masses were kept happy by endless military parades, glittering sabres and horses nodding and prancing to the music of the band. But underneath it all, the arts, that barometer of the human spirit, began to register febrile excesses and signs of decadence. A form of pornography began to infiltrate refined taste. It was not the roistering obscenity of Rabelais but something much more cloistered, more perverse and bilious.

The sickening of the arts was a symptom that a whole series of fragile bubbles would sooner or later burst releasing decay, destruction and war.

The First World War was sparked off by the rash act of yet another of the innumerable student terrorists who had made a sport of dispatching ministers, presidents, and crowned heads to a premature death. In fact, of course, assassins are often scapegoats for much larger movements which are searching for an excuse for conflict.

Austria-Hungary was, at the time, an Empire created of a multitude of disparate elements: Czechs, Slovaks, Slovenians, Croats, Bosnians, with Romanian and many other minorities, speaking different languages and having different traditions.

The Crown Prince of Austria went on a tour of inspection of the provinces of Bosnia-Herzegovina in the summer of 1914 for a very good reason. He was annoyed. Serbia, despite its antagonism to Austria-Hungary, and its protection by its big Slav sister, Russia, was in the habit of buying its armaments from Skoda, the great arms factory in present-day Czechoslovakia, in which the Crown Prince was one of the principal shareholders. Suddenly Serbia, in the light of the increasing possibility of future conflict, began to wonder if it was really wise to

Tsar Nicholas and his Tsarina, Alexandra, wearing traditional Russian costume for a fancy dress ball.

The Imperial family

purchase weapons from a potential enemy, and went unexpectedly to Schneider-Creusot in France for its supply.

The Crown Prince was incensed, not only as an heir to a throne, but as a businessman. He retaliated by hitting Serbia where it hurt her most: he halted the importation of Serbian pigs into Austria. In Sarajevo, against a background of guns, pigs and provocation, the Archduke of Austria, Franz Ferdinand, was shot dead.

This dignified pretext was all that Europe had been waiting for. It unleashed a wave of jingoism and plunged Europe into the most terrible war in history. After a series of demands and ultimata, the Austrians, prompted by the Germans, declared war on Serbia on 28 June 1914. Russia ordered partial mobilization. The next day Germany jumped the gun by declaring war on Russia, and while she was about it, on France as well, hoping, as Hitler was to do later, for British neutrality. On 31 July, Russia ordered general mobilization, and once again limping autocracy was saved by patriotic fervour. On 1 August, Russia and Germany were at war. On 4 August, German troops entered Belgium,

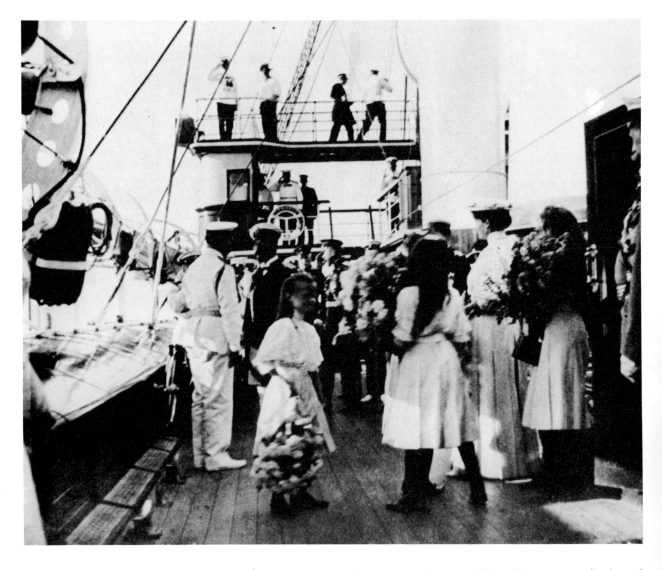

A meeting of Emperors: Tsar Nicholas II and the Imperial family on board Kaiser Wilhelm's yacht.

and at midnight of the same day a British ultimatum expired, and Britain was consequently at war with Germany.

The old photographs of these light-hearted mobilizations are eloquent of the nations' high hopes for a brief and brilliant war. God was on everyone's side, but eventually on no one's. There was talk of the war being over by Christmas, as though it would be played to the umpire's whistle. Men, drunk with adrenaline or liquor, clung to the outside of railway carriages, waving bottles or straw hats. On the trains were cheerful messages in chalk, *Nach Paris, A Berlin*. They couldn't both be right. They could, however, both be wrong.

It is curiously sad to follow the sudden darkening of the landscape in English social magazines like *Sphere* or *The Tatler*. The outbreak of hostilities is hardly mentioned, and only very demurely is a new note struck. The oval photographs of four uppercrust lovelies are garlanded with floral designs to make a handsome page. Three of them are engaged to be married. The husband of the fourth has been posted missing. Judging from her radiant features, he's bound to turn up sooner or later.

Then, when warships began to be sunk by German submarines, there was a kind of remote awareness and a sudden sense of outrage, as though there had been cheating during a sporting encounter. As the pain of war began to be felt, the first grotesque caricatures of the German Kaiser began to appear, spittle dislodging itself in showers from his wolfish molars as he prepares to make an *hors d'oeuvre* of gallant little Belgium, impaled on his massive fork and dressed in a vaguely Flemish national costume.

Russia had no time for such a gradual introduction to war. After all, unlike Britain it was not an island. Russia mobilized with extraordinary rapidity, and thrust two armies into East Prussia, the First under Rennenkampf, a general who had distinguished himself in the rather more intimate area of chasing Socialists, and the Second under Samsonov. Although ill prepared and untried, the Russian pincer attack succeeded in routing the Germans and the German commander, von Prittwitz, was replaced by the formidable combination of Hindenburg and Ludendorff.

A photograph of a regiment of Cossacks in 1914. According to the *Illustrated War News* in which this photograph was reproduced, 'A patrol of ten Cossacks came upon a squadron of German cavalry who dismounted and opened fire to avoid a hand-to-hand encounter. The Cossacks, as they attacked, swung themselves beneath their horses' girths in their favourite style. The trick deceived the Germans, who mounted to ride after what they supposed to be riderless horses. Thereupon the Cossacks suddenly reappeared in the saddle and cut them to pieces.'

The Russian Army had by now acquired field radios despite the earlier opposition to all electronic aids, but they seemed unable to imagine that anyone could listen to their conversations, which the Germans did to their evident gain.

By some highly successful manoeuvres, and superior intelligence, the Germans managed to keep the two Russian armies apart, and dealt with them one after the other despite their considerable numerical inferiority. Samsonov's Second Army was annihilated at the Battle of Tannenberg, and its Commander committed suicide on the field. Rennenkampf, now alone, retreated from German soil. This early disaster cost Russia the loss of a quarter-of-a-million men and much equipment, but it did afford the French and her allies a breathing-space on the Western Front, from where two entire German army corps had been transferred.

In the south, the Austrians fared less happily. After some initial successes, they were driven back, and a breach of their line was threatened. Once again the Germans came to the rescue, parrying and thrusting in order to thwart the much vaunted Russian steam-roller which, using sheer manpower, was seeking an all-out victory. As winter advanced, it became obvious that the undeveloped armament industry was physically incapable of supplying this gargantuan but primitive military machine with even a fraction of its needs, and a stalemate set in there as in the West. Men sat, lethally bored in wet trenches, immobile except for the occasional piece of bravura, like patients waiting in the anteroom of hell.

1915 saw no end to this war of attrition with the entry of Turkey on the side of the Central Powers and Italy on the side of the Allies.

The Germans, unable to see a solution to the stalemate in the West, turned their attention to a general offensive in the East hoping, together

Tsar Nicholas II blessing his troops with an icon.

Hospital workers being inspected by Tsar Nicholas II during the First World War.

with their Austrian allies, to knock Russia out of the war once and for all. The Russian Commander-in-Chief, Grand Duke Nicholas, succeeded, by dint of able generalship, in saving the body of his armies, despite the loss of the whole of Poland and three-quarters-of-a-million prisoners to add to the almost half a million lost the previous year.

Von Falkenhayn, the new German Chief-of-Staff, believed that Russia was so shattered by these losses that the time had come to turn his attentions exclusively towards the West.

In June 1916, co-ordinating their efforts with the Allied offensive on the Somme, the Russians under General Brusilov showed themselves still able to launch a surprise attack on the Austrians which quickly made headway. Some 200,000 Austrian prisoners were taken in the course of the first three days. The situation was so perilous that German troops had to be diverted from the Western Front in order to stop the rot. Von Falkenhayn was replaced by Hindenburg, and Romania, encouraged by Russian victories, entered the war on the Allied side.

Despite early successes, Romania was quickly overrun by German and Bulgarian troops, her oil and wheat falling into the Central Power's kitty, while the Russian Front was lengthened by 500 kilometres. Brusilov's efforts extended into 1917, but by now the cancer which had been gnawing at Russia's entrails ever since the principles of autocracy had outlived their time, struck at vital organs of the nation. The decline was accelerated not only by the enormous sacrifices of the Russian people, with roughly a million dead, but also by the repulsive silliness of the Tsar's entourage. The Tsarina, a woman of majestic insensitivity, told her husband to get rid of Stürmer, the Prime Minister. With his German name he was bound to be pro-German. It was Rasputin who told her what to do, and the direction of the war was dictated by his casual whims. At his command the Tsarina sent an apple to the Tsar which had been blessed by a bedridden abbess with a reputation for supernatural gifts. In her letters, the Tsarina begged for confirmation that the Tsar had eaten the apple, since it would ensure an upswing in the Empire's military fortunes. At last the Tsar was able to state that

Nicholas II at General Headquarters

The Tsar reviewing the Seminovsky Regiment.

The Tsar with the Supreme Commander, Grand Duke Nicholas, on the Eastern Front.

the sanctified apple had indeed been received, and devoutly consumed. But, as in the garden of Eden, things went from bad to worse.

The Tsar was at the front, having taken over the Supreme Command from the surprisingly competent Grand Duke Nicholas. A worse choice could not have been made, even by the Tsar.

The Duma pleaded for a really national government, representing all opinions. The result was the expulsion of all ministers in favour of a national government. Courageous relatives and foreign diplomats pleaded with the Tsar, bringing to his attention the serious possibility of revolution if the temper of the nation was not heeded. Even quite reputable and previously conciliatory personalities began to agitate and even to plot. General Krymov spread the idea of a necessary palace revolution as early as 1916, and it seems certain that some liberal and progressive ministers were ready to form an emergency cabinet in the event of the plot's success. Even the successful General Brusilov appears to have been party to the conspiracy while he was actively waging war, and to have given it the stamp of his approval.

General Krymov wished to force the abdication of the Tsar in favour of the sickly Tsarevich, with a regency under the Grand Duke Mikhail, and the appointment of new and effective ministers. The plot was delayed and finally rendered obsolete by the dramatic events of a more far-reaching revolution.

The revolution began with strikes which had nothing directly to do with authority, but more to do with hunger and basic human needs. Several baker's shops were looted, and the police were intent merely on keeping the demonstrators out of the city centre. The milling crowds began to develop an ugly mood, and were joined by groups of students. Once students were involved, a few isolated threats to autocracy were bound to be heard.

On 10 March, the crowd consolidated, and grew bold. Several police stations were occupied. The crowd took courage. Amazingly, the Cossacks, usually objects of terror, behaved in a friendly fashion, and even encouraged the strikers. The Tsar, from headquarters, instructed the military governor to suppress the rising. Detachments of guards and police cadets moved obediently against the strikers. Shots were fired. There were many dead. The news spread. Then a spontaneous sense of outrage spilled over, and with a sense of emotional release the soldiers of several crack regiments joined the strikers. A force of reliable troops was sent to arrest the mutineers. Face to face, they fraternized. The revolution had begun, a spontaneous, leaderless combustion of popular sentiment, of hunger, of weariness, and finally of enthusiasm.

The Tsar was reduced to sending from the Front, troops who were uninfluenced by these urban events, to put down the rebellion. The government, which had no more reserves of power, had to wait nervously until these troops arrived. It attempted to continue as though nothing had happened, at first within the Winter Palace, then at the Admiralty,

Cars attacked by revolutionaries on the streets of St Petersburg in March 1917.

A remarkable still from a film made at the time of the storming of the Winter Palace in 1917.

but finally it went underground, after which its members were arrested individually.

In the popular imagination, the revolution swept aside established power in a trice, changing the form of government in a stroke by over-throwing the Tsar, and replacing him by Lenin. The official Marxist account of the Revolution irons out events and paints the revolution-aries as infallible in their prescience. While they are glorified, opposi-tion, even within revolutionary ranks, is blackened at the expense of credibility. History is, by its nature, as untidy as the present.

The revolution was not a decisive moment, but rather yet another lingering agony, relieved only by a variety of hopes. The populace, intoxicated by its unexpected victory, and hoping to keep up its momen-tum, asked the Duma to assume responsibilities which had been denied it in the past. It is difficult to become democratic all at once after having been constrained merely to present a façade of democracy for so long, and the Duma hesitated. It sent an urgent message to the Tsar begging him to make concessions to popular demands in order to save the monarchy. The Tsar refused to take the warning seriously. Meanwhile the troops sent to suppress the revolution had met with their first, and indeed last, obstacle when the railway workers flatly refused to transport them to the capital.

On 12 March the first Soviet Committee held what was an orderly yet intermittently tumultuous meeting to take decisions to do with defence and the supply of food. The Soviet consisted of Socialist members of the Strike Committee, and various workers' delegates from all branches of industry, including the influential munitions makers.

The Congress was frequently interrupted as representatives of newly defected regiments pledged their allegiance to the revolution against a background of frenetic cheers.

Then, at last, the Duma moved, and agreed on the formation of a new government. Perhaps surprisingly, this news was greeted with enthusiasm by the leaders of the Soviet. There has been conjecture as to why a popular assembly, heady with victory, should have greeted the resumption of a bourgeois administration with such enthusiasm when it seemed to have powers within its grasp. One reason must certainly have been that its job was not government, but administration, the solving of the palpable problems of the day, and the fortification of a simple bastion. It was not ready to assume responsibility for either foreign affairs or the direction of the war. Several regiments had indeed joined forces with them, but the true temper of the army on distant fronts could merely be guessed at. They were not ready to be responsible for the whole body of Russia in one afternoon when they had not had time fully to digest the head. The Duma could govern, but under surveillance from below. And it would not be able to undo what already had been done. It suited the revolutionaries to have a figurehead.

The first question on the agenda was a thorny one. Realizing that the point of no return had been reached after centuries of grand phrases about autocracy, two conservative members of the Duma were dispatched to Pskov, Imperial headquarters, in order to demand the Tsar's abdication in favour of his son. The autocrat, so florid in his Edicts, proved eminently reasonable in conversation. He declined to place the inhuman weight of Tsardom on the shoulders of his infirm son, and offered their double abdication in favour of the Grand Duke Mikhail. At the same time, he asked for safe passage for his family and himself to Great Britain, where he had relatives. When this news leaked out, the Soviet ordered his arrest. Whoever governed, it was clear where the power lay.

The great question now was what to do about the appalling sacrifices being made to continue the war. The government was for a continuance of the war, since it saw no dignified alternative. The Soviet, on the other hand, saw no future in this fighting of a bourgeois war for the preservation of outdated values, in which the common man of every nation was being disgracefully butchered for the convenience of the ruling classes. It issued a manifesto only just over two weeks after its first meeting, declaring that Russia had no territorial ambitions whatsoever, and was willing to conclude peace with her enemies on a basis of no changes in territorial demarcation lines and no indemnities. It even issued instructions to the many military and naval committees that the orders of the government need only be obeyed if they conformed with the orders of the Soviet. Strict discipline while on duty was required, but off-duty saluting was abolished, as was the complicated protocol of addressing officers by courtesy titles. Officers in their turn were expressly forbidden to use the patronizing second person singular in speaking to other ranks.

The wretched government had never been its own master. Either it had been the unwilling mouthpiece of the group of sinister fools clinging to the raft of autocracy, or else, as now, it was the figurehead for something new and frightening.

On 19 April the government was made to issue a statement to the effect that Russia desired nothing more than a permanent peace based on the self-determination of all peoples. In case this should frighten her allies, Milyutin, the Foreign Minister, sent soothing messages to assure leaders in all allied capitals that Russia had every intention of pursuing the war.

The revelation of this duplicity caused new tension between the Soviet and the government, and it was deemed necessary to include five members of the Soviet in the government because, as the Minister for War eloquently put it, 'Some are fully responsible without an ounce of power, others retain full power without a trace of responsibility.'

This new coalition was faced with insuperable difficulties, and decided, in a manner which seemed wildly gallant or utterly half-witted, according to divergent points of view, to add voluntarily to the

Kerensky in 1917 when Minister of War in the provisional Government.

Workers with an armoured car which
they had seized from Kerensky.

difficulties as a way of solving them. It was as though an Olympic high-
jumper had decided to attempt the world record without bothering
about any of the lesser heights. Russia seemed to dare itself to do the
impossible. In spite of the utter demoralization of the army in the
field, a large-scale offensive was now decided on, presumably on the
assumption that such a piece of braggadocio would show the world
that there was life in the old dog yet.

Kerensky, the new Minister of War, an orator of some power, went
himself to the Front, and harangued the troops with appeals for a
miracle. Nothing less would be acceptable. The troops applauded his
rhetoric, and when he had gone, piled up their empty rifles, and refused
to join in the offensive. Quite a few units were disbanded for mutiny.

The attack took place on 1 July 1917, and met with some success until
29 July, by when it had not only been halted, but the last vestiges of
cohesion had disappeared, and Russia lay defenceless before her
enemies.

It would take more than the ephemeral tirades of a gifted lawyer to
stem the tide, and give the nation the possibility of healing its wounds.

Vladimir Ilich Ulyanov, known as Lenin, had spent most of his
recent life in exile. As early as 1 November 1914, he had issued a
manifesto denouncing the Great War as an Imperialist conflict in
which all parties were equally guilty. As so often with movements of the
left, the main scorn is vented not on creatures of the right, who are what
they are because of economic circumstances, but on those slightly less
to the left, people who speak ringingly of the ideas of universalism and
justice for all, but who at the first note of a distant bugle go scampering
off to follow this or that flag to fratricidal disaster. He saw the world
divided laterally into classes, and not horizontally into nations, and
that a true great war, if ever it was fought, should be between the
workers and those who pull the strings.

Anarchism, too, was an enemy, since it weakened the clear obligations of the working class and its perceptions of things as they are. It
clouded the vision, softened the focus, confused. All faculties were
required, with burning clarity, to settle the job at hand. His mind was
objective, his resolve grim, and his conviction unblemished by doubt,
which did not prevent him from being a subtle diplomatist if circumstances required it.

When the first revolution broke out, he was in Switzerland. He
immediately tried to return to Russia by way of England. It was against
British interests to let him through. He then decided to go through
Germany, which led emigré opinion to believe subsequently that his
arrival was part of a devilish plot of the German General Staff to
undermine Russian morale. Hindsight is not only responsible for
retarded wisdom but, in some cases, for the creation of convenient
legends. For Lenin, Germany was no more an enemy than England

France, or Russia itself, and, by the same token, no more a friend. His determination was to reach Russia at all cost now that the avalanche had begun of its own accord. One man alone could not have started it, but now that it was a reality, there was a possibility of dominating the many tendencies making up the Soviet even if Lenin's party, the Bolsheviks, were only sparsely represented. History was to demonstrate yet again that the real enemies of the left are others of the left. The question of policy is never as open to contention as the question of degree.

Today, outside the Finland Station in Leningrad, there is a large statue of Lenin making a declaration, before which newlyweds like to have themselves photographed. Within the station itself, the engine

Lenin (1870–1924).

which pulled his train is encased in glass. The impression is given of a triumphal arrival on 3 April 1917.

Lenin did, in fact, make a speech in the station. He declared that the arrest of the Tsar was merely a preliminary step in the main struggle, which was to dissociate Soviet power entirely from a collaboration with the bourgeoisie. The present revolution, tainted with compromise, could not for long satisfy the proletariat. It needed a mobilization of the provinces to seize power totally in the name of Socialism.

The speech did not go down too well, especially with those who saw in compromise the only practical solution. Even some Bolsheviks were depressed by the lack of pragmatism displayed by their leader in his unswerving idealism. The old Bolshevik theorist, Plekhanov, went as far as to characterize the speech as mad. But Lenin foresaw instinctively in which direction the tide was carrying the nation, and guessed that his diatribe was merely a little ahead of its time. His newspaper, *Pravda*, the Truth, despite its very limited circulation was being read by more and more people. He was becoming a real threat to those devoted to salvaging what they could from the old order.

Kerensky, whose elevated sentiments had inspired the troops to both applause and inaction, had now been rewarded by the Premiership. Under his aegis, forged documents were published on 5 July, proving that Lenin was merely a paid puppet of the German General Staff. That same evening, troops marched from the Front and some Cadets entered the city, and sought to crush the Soviets. Lenin was forced to take refuge, at first in a worker's home, then in Finland. Trotsky, Kamenev and Lunacharsky were imprisoned, and the printing press of the *Pravda* was destroyed by the mob. The violence in the streets merely strengthened the resolve of the Soviets, and pushed them towards extremism, which is exactly what Lenin had foreseen. The Soviets of both the capital and Moscow voted in a Bolshevik majority for the first time. Lenin repeated his famous dictum, *Tipyer ili nikagda!* (Now or never) in inflammatory articles and broadsheets.

On 27 October, after over three months in hiding, he reappeared, and from his simple room in the Smolny Institute, once a finishing school for daughters of the nobility, he took over the direction of the Second Congress of the Soviets.

But with all his resolve, one fact had been proved yet again. However many changes there were at the top, the problems remained, as demanding of resolution as ever. Not only were the Germans and Austrians still in the field, and advancing in places, but there was complete chaos in the countryside, where the massacre of the landed gentry and the burning of stately homes was the order of the day. There was wanton destruction of everything even vaguely symbolic of existing order, such as forests and rolling-stock, while groups of deserters pillaged and looted. Since the struggle for power was at last concentrated in the capital, Petrograd,

The villa in Finland where Lenin hid from Russian authorities in 1917 before the October Revolution.

there was neither the energy nor the will, let alone the capability, to deal with the total collapse of authority.

Soon the Germans appeared in Estonia, occupying the Island of Osel, and threatening the approaches to the capital. Kerensky wished to transfer the government to Moscow, a symptom of panic which suited the resolute Bolsheviks down to the ground. The government was accused of treason, and on 26 October, Trotsky and the Soviet formed a military Revolutionary Committee, ostensibly for the defence of the capital.

On 3 November, Trotsky demanded of the General Staff that all its orders should be countersigned by a responsible member of this Committee. Not unnaturally, the General Staff, clutching at shreds of illusory dignity, declined. The next day, a meeting of Revolutionary delegates representing the army passed a resolution which replaced obedience to the orders of the General Staff by allegiance to the Committee. The day after, Kerensky issued an ultimatum, requiring a withdrawal of the offending resolution. He received no acknowledgment, so he raised the bridges in order to hinder communications, and demanded dictatorial powers to cope with the situation. These were accorded after an exhausting all-night session, but before anything concrete could be

Soldiers take to the streets in support of
the October Revolution.

done, the Bolsheviks seized all government offices, including the headquarters of the telephone network. Kerensky immediately left for the
Front by an American Embassy car in order to scour for a few reliable
regiments to help reimpose his constitutional authority on the revolutionaries. After a few unhelpful meetings with depressed generals who
were having a difficult enough time holding the Germans, he found a
more attentive listener in General Krasnov, who commanded some
Cossacks. Four days later, the Cossacks were within sight of the capital,
and their precipitate advance encouraged the conservative elements in
the tattered government to order the arrest of the Revolutionary Military Committee. They could not imagine that a rabble of other ranks
could possibly stand up to Cossacks under the leadership of a general.
As usual, they were wrong. By early afternoon, with the help of the
cruiser, *Aurora*, and some sailors of the Baltic fleet, it was all over.
General Krasnov eventually surrendered and Kerensky fled. The rest
of the government were arrested. Then the real work began.

The enthusiasm was contagious. Despite some disturbances and
exchanges of fire in Moscow and other large cities, the Soviets, under
their slogans and rippling banners, managed to impose their authority
on the country in a mere three weeks. The platform of the dictatorship
of the proletariat captured the imagination of even those who did not
quite understand what it entailed. In many ways, the idealism of these
early days was touching, especially when the Revolutionaries began to
realize the extent of their achievement. They extended a fraternal hand
across the frontiers from what they saw as the glow of hope surrounding
them into the tenebrous night of the capitalist world, with its glaring
inequalities and war-weariness. These were the days when the worker

of the world were supposed to unite, and follow Russia's example in a Utopian surge towards liberty, equality and fraternity. For once Russia was ahead of the game. She had something to teach, not merely herself (that she had done before), but the world! There was nothing subversive about this call, it was an innocent cry of one who has found a way out of the labyrinth to the others lost within.

We can still sense a pained surprise that others did not heed the call with the expected alacrity. But this was not a time for idealism. The Germans were still advancing. There were armies still at the front, without sufficient guns, and for those guns, little or no ammunition. In many cases, the bayonet was the only effective weapon. As Suvorov had said in happier times, 'The bullet's a fool; the bayonet's a clever fellow.' Now the Russians had a chance to prove the dictum, even if a German army in 1917 was a vastly different proposition from Napoleon's galloping horsemen.

Lenin realized that his first duty towards his own country was to sue for peace, however humiliating, however debasing it should turn out to

In 1918, members of the 6th Soviet Congress at the unveiling of a memorial in Red Square to commemorate those who had fallen in the October Revolution of the previous year.

The storming of the Winter Palace.

be. Russia was in no position to continue the struggle and, in any case, it was a struggle of which Lenin heartily disapproved. On 9 November, Trotsky invited all powers engaged in the conflict to conclude an armistice prior to the ending of hostilities. The Allied governments expressed their opposition to this move at once, and spoke earnestly to the new Chief of the Armed Forces, General Dukhonin. He was dismissed for lending an ear to these complaints, and subsequently killed by his own troops. The suspicion began to grow among the Allies, which by now included the Americans, that Lenin was more than likely in the pay of Germany.

The banks, which were still private, and obviously shared the Allied opinion, refused to finance the changes undertaken by the Bolsheviks. Lenin nationalized them with the stroke of a pen, decreed that the land automatically belonged to those who worked it, free of rent, and proclaimed an eight-hour day for workers. Whenever a hole appeared in the fabric, the Soviet plugged it, and very quickly. Owing to the refusal of the various organs of free enterprise to cooperate, the state took over almost every facet of business and manufacture, though having neither the experience nor the technical knowledge to do half that which expediency dictated.

The peace negotiations with the Germans began just before Christmas, 1917 in the town of Brest Litovsk, and almost immediately, became evident that the terms imposed on the Russians would be brutal

Independence was demanded for Poland, the Baltic States, Finland and even for the Ukraine. Trotsky countered the German demands by attempting to have the best of both worlds by a strange arabesque. While turning down the terms put forward, he nevertheless declared hostilities to be over. The Germans exploded the Russians' wishful thinking by continuing to advance. Lenin decided the Treaty would have to be signed, but he met stiff resistance from Soviet Revolutionaries and others represented in the Soviet. There were those, and many of them, who could not bear to entertain thoughts of a virtual surrender – Trotsky's pipe-dream of 'neither peace nor war' did not seem to make much practical sense – and who deemed that too many lives had been lost heroically for even the addled fruit of such successes to be thrown away gratuitously.

Lenin won the day, but not without difficulty, as ever astonished by the capacity for sentimentality in dedicated leftwingers. Acting independently, the Ukraine had accepted German overlordship; other national minorities were clamouring for independence; a 'White' Army

adets in the captured Winter Palace

was forming in Manchuria; the Japanese threatened to occupy Vlad vostok and the Germans demanded a huge indemnity. Despite all the inconveniences, Lenin, through his Commissar for Foreign Affairs, t aristocratic Chicherin, who had spent some time in British gao was able to reach a final accommodation with the German delegates c 3 March 1918.

The Germans undertook, for their part, not to transfer troo relieved from service on the Eastern Front to the Western Front, a agreement which they broke forthwith. At the same time Trotsky w intimating to the British and Americans that the Treaty might never ratified if the Soviet was able to count on Allied aid, especially in t Far East, but also against German incursions. At first the Allies seeme well disposed towards these overtures, but they had not yet recovere from their initial shock at the separate peace, and must have aske themselves how reliable these overtures were. In any case, from t behaviour of both parties to the Treaty it would be judged that it w an accommodation of convenience, which was not destined to survi that convenience. In the absence of Allied assurances, the Treaty w ratified on 16 March.

Lenin did not waste his time. He worked feverishly to train a viak administration and to organize both the economy and the milita capacity of the nation, which despite its exhaustion was now fired by a *esprit de corps* quite different to that of its paternalistic past.

One effect of this unique upheaval was that all those affected by were reduced to guesswork instead of precedents, and not unnaturall they all guessed wrong. Lenin was absolutely convinced that the tir for a world revolution of the proletariat had come, and the Allies we equally convinced that the Bolshevik uprising was a flash in the pa which could never survive against external and internal pressure Every event which occurred at this time must be seen in the light of tl double misapprehension.

Large scale sabotage was the current means of protest against t State, and discontent was growing, especially in rural communitie The peasants had been delighted when told that the land belonged he who works it. They now discovered that he who works it only wor it on behalf of a greedy government, which confiscates any produ deemed excessive for his own needs. This may have been the result bitter expediency, but it was far too reminiscent of the bad old days.

Counter-revolutionaries even succeeded in occupying the town Yaroslavl, only 300 kilometres away from Moscow. They were blood suppressed.

Rumours abounded in the West, a mixture of wishful thinking a melodrama predominating. It was known that as many as 45,000 Cze deserters from the Austro-Hungarian Army had been preparing f some time in Siberia to join the Russian Imperial Army in an attempt

ABOVE: The interior of a Moscow theatre in 1856.
BELOW LEFT: Tchaikovsky in 1893 by N. Kuznetsov.
BELOW RIGHT: Leo Tolstoy at work in 1884 by N. N. Gey.

茲ニ戦敷設水雷ニ觸
露戦闘旗艦兼
沈シ司令提督マカ
ロフ中將溺死ス

マカロフ中將

free their country. Now, at the outset of civil war, Trotsky tried to disarm the Czechs. They resisted. It came to clashes with Bolshevik levies, in which the Russians were no match for the highly organized Czechs. By the end of July, the Czechs had set up a government of their own in Siberia, with the tacit encouragement of the Allies, and began a westward march to defeat Soviet power in Europe. As they neared Ekaterinburg, where the Tsar and his family were in custody, the local Soviet, in evident fear of losing their distinguished prisoners, voted to destroy them. Citizen Romanov and his family were executed on the night of 16 July. No trace of them or their belongings was ever found. Ten years later, a woman claimed to be the Grand Duchess Anastasia who had escaped the slaughter. This was, of course, in the best Russian tradition, as was the fact that nobody ever found out the truth.

Encouraged by the Czech successes, and those of Admiral Kolchak at the head of a 'White' Army, and appalled, as constitutional democracies always are by the death of despots, the Allies decided to intervene militarily in Russian affairs. A British Expeditionary Force landed at Murmansk, on the White Sea, and occupied Archangel on 2 August. They set up a provisional government after unseating the local Soviet. Then, as had been threatened, an entire Japanese division took Vladivostok, accompanied by substantial French and British contingents, and two United States regiments from their base on the Philippines. Within a month, after several seemingly decisive engagements, the whole of Siberia was virtually in the hands of Anti-Soviet forces, while the British were advancing southward from the Arctic Circle to effect a junction with the main force crossing the Urals. The French landed at Odessa. Other Allied forces arrived in the Caucasus. The Ukraine was under the hegemony of the pro-German puppet, Herman Skoropadsky. It looked as though the end was near for the impertinent amateurs in Moscow, who had the vanity to think they could improvize the running of an Empire, who defied international banking procedure and shot those to whom they owed allegiance. Over 150,000 soldiers were closing in on them, and soon their subversive communications with the enemy would cease. The ringleaders would be exemplarily punished and once more an acceptable government would be installed to everybody's advantage.

It is difficult to overestimate the effects of this intervention at a time when Russia's revolution was regarded as a defeat for morality. She lay, an apparently mortally wounded dinosaur, as huge and impractical as a prehistoric animal which had, by some fluke of nature, survived into modern times. Now the vultures were settling on her warm body, and finding her flesh to their liking. It is even more difficult to overestimate the effect when the dinosaur rose unexpectedly, shook the vultures off, and struck at them clumsily. The landscape was full of feathers.

During the Russo-Japanese War of 1904–5 the Russian flagship was sunk in the Straits of Tsushima as this Japanese illustration records.

CHAPTER THIRTEEN

Pragmatism, Heresy and Anti-Semitism

Ironically, it was the Allies' success in the war which helped to undermine the Allies' success in Russia. The new Bolshevik armies savaged the Czechs, and halted the White armies. The Czechs wanted to go home, and lost their interest in the complications of Russian internal quarrels. The Allies reinforced their armies, but in the West, Germany began to crumble, as did Turkey. The whole structure of the Central Powers was menaced, and a revolt, if not a revolution, broke out among German sailors, and Lenin thought it a vindication of all his policies. Before this, however, there had been changes in the temper of the Soviet government itself.

On 30 August 1918, a girl called Dora Kaplan made an attempt on Lenin's life. She was one of the Social Revolutionaries opposed to the separate peace with Germany. On 31 August, Uritsky, Chief of the Secret Police, was also shot. Uritsky died, Lenin lived. Nearly one thousand people suspected of complicity in these acts or having sympathy with them, were executed in Moscow and Petrograd. The terror had begun, as it had done during the French Revolution, and as apparently it always must when the momentum of a movement is lost, and the practical difficulties begin crowding in. This time the terror was dubbed Red, not to confuse it with the original of the French Revolution.

The Soviet, with control of the railways, and shorter lines of communication, gradually began to erode the initial advantages of their opponents. General Yudenich, operating from Estonia, with the help of tanks supplied by Britain, had managed to get to within 15 kilometres of Petrograd, but Denikin and later Wrangel were pushed back in the south. The Allies, frustrated, evacuated Russian soil without succeeding in having imposed their will or left anything apart from some destruction and many bitter memories. The expansionist Japanese lingered on for another year or two in the Far East.

Meanwhile Trotsky devised a plan for utilizing the mobilization for the benefits of both agriculture and industry, despite the scepticism of Lenin and the opposition of trades unions. This employment of soldiers for so many jobs away from the barrack square was received with signs of anger by both the military and the workers, but it did help to start wrecked factories up again and mend the fences. Overseas, it spread the suspicion that Russia was disguising a refusal to demobilize as other

Lenin speaks. A contemporary poster.

Stalin, Lenin and Kalinin at the Party's Congress in 1919

countries were doing, and that this army would, at a given moment, abandon its ploughshares and its anvils, take up arms again, and commit further mischief. The fact that powerful internationalist armies had come to grief against untried Bolshevik commanders like Frunze, heading troops who improvized their tactics, did nothing to reassure the West that Russia was not just simulating exhaustion, distress, and surrender, and it was feared she would drop the mask and start new adventures, now that everyone else was really worn out.

Admittedly Estonia, Latvia, Lithuania and Poland had regained their independence, but elsewhere parts of Germany and Austria were struggling against Communist insurrection, while Hungary actually had a short-lived Communist government under Bela Kun. Russia offered a peace treaty to Poland, under generous terms, which included parts of Byelorussia and Western Ukraine. Thus Poland became an independent reality once again for the first time since her partition at the time of Catherine the Great. The revived *cordon sanitaire* deserved every encouragement as a buffer against the perplexing giant whose altruism was as suspect to the West as its motives were veiled. As an encouragement, France presented Poland with extensive war material. The United States gave something perhaps even more appreciated, a loan of $50,000,000, ostensibly for food purchases. It was quite like old times. Poland remembered in a trice the great power she had been, and presumably also remembered the chaotic land Russia had been in the 'Time of Troubles', when Polish kings had been invited to rule over her, *faute de mieux*.

The Poles turned back the clock, and in a paroxysm of national pride, demanded the restitution of their eighteenth-century frontier, a large

The agit train which travelled round the country 'educating' the people about the Revolution. A photograph taken in 1919.

The cover of *The Communist International* published in Russia in 1919 for worldwide distribution.

sum of money, and the Russian city of Smolensk as a final twist of the knife. The Russians considered that independence was an adequate gift in itself, and the Poles consequently invaded the Ukraine, occupying Kiev in June. There was a violent Soviet counter-attack, which not only retook Kiev, but which found itself in the outskirts of Warsaw within two months.

This was not at all in the West's interests, and French staff officers under Weygand brilliantly redressed the balance, helping the Poles to advance their border. The new Poland included a Russian minority of about four million, for which she was destined to pay a heavy price later on.

The West breathed more easily again; in fact Romania was able to take Bessarabia back. It looked as though the Russians were once again fenced in to their prairie, and the vacuum caused by the German collapse was slowly filling with Western air. Lenin, in declining health, had been finally disappointed in his ambitions for world revolution, and was entirely obsessed with internal problems. Russia, which had taken

Lenin addressing the 2nd Congress of Comintern in 1920.

An informal photograph of Stalin and
Lenin in 1922

so long to impose her influence as a great power; which had been largely
instrumental in the defeat of Napoleon and was the salvation of France
and Switzerland under Alexander I; which had played a leading part in
European affairs as a protector of Slav peoples in the Balkans, and as a
leading dancer in the gavotte of nations; which had added new perceptions to the human condition through her literature, was now back in the
isolation ward. She was led by people who were learning their jobs the
hard way. Nevertheless, they had proved that they could be dangerous,
that they could defeat armies unexpectedly, while revising accepted
values of behaviour.

One of Lenin's last actions was to institute the New Economic Policy
of 1921. It was the result of pragmatism, a realization that the system

which had inevitably tightened under the impact of endless conflict now desperately needed ventilation and relaxation. He also realized that there was a certain romanticism in the glorification of a proletarian revolution in a country with relatively few industries and a great mass of illiterate peasants. The revolution only spread to the country; it was animated by the cities, and Moscow in particular.

The New Economic Policy offered incentives to foreign investment while making private business transactions legal. Private individuals were permitted to own limited industrial enterprises, and to be involved in the retail trade. The grain surpluses were no longer expropriated by the State, but could be sold in the market. The leasing of labour or of land was permitted on a controlled scale.

To many Communist diehards, this seemed like heresy. The visionaries, once opposed by the clergy and the boyars, were now opposed by the patriots of the Communist Party. Throughout her tortured history, Russia has always been cursed by those for whom the letter of the law is immutable, instead of being as changeable as the seasons, which create as they destroy, giving life and death, but never a living death.

With the death of Lenin, after several incapacitating strokes, we enter a period within the lucid living memory of some, and it is perhaps time to take stock of a tendency which has added fuel to the fire of prejudice throughout the ages.

It is that of anti-semitism, a phenomenon of which it is difficult to speak objectively, so sensitive has the issue become largely owing to the unspeakable barbarism of Hitler, but also, more recently by the emergence of a Zionist state which has turned into militancy the pious reticence of centuries. Historically, the attitude to Jews in Russia had been not much different to that of other European states, with the exception that in Russia, popular Jewish culture became more immediately identified with the Russians all around them. It is conceivable that some antagonisms were due to the very proximity of the two modes of life in things that really mattered. In any Jewish restaurant, for instance, blintzers turn up on the table, which are none other than what the Russians call blini, together with salted cucumbers, and other staple products of Russian cuisine. It is indicative that Russia and Germany, the two countries identified in the popular imagination and insistent propaganda with anti-semitism, are those which had the greatest influence on the domestic habits of the Jews. There was no comparative French, English or other influence.

The charming story is told of Levi Eshkol, a recent President of Israel, who used not only to fall asleep during public functions, but even talk in his sleep. When this occurred, the language he used was invariably Russian. His wife chided him, and begged him to make every effort to speak Hebrew under these circumstances, since his habit, innocuous enough in itself, created a bad impression.

The elite in Israel at the time of writing is almost exclusively Russian or Polish in origin, which sometimes gives the impression that the creation of the State is much like a heart transplant, with an anxious world waiting to see if the body will accept the heart, or attempt to reject it. There can be little doubt that if the elite was Sephardic (Mediterranean) instead of Ashkenazic, if it were not the product of centuries of oppression under completely foreign circumstances, an accommodation with the Arabs would be much easier and less abrasive.

The anti-semitism of the Russian state set up its own reaction within the country. As early as the reign of Elizabeth in the eighteenth century, Jewish traders were barred from the Empire despite the ardent pleas of Russian merchants that such additions to the Russian market place were good for business. Behind every restrictive practice lay the usual villains of the piece, the Church and the nobles at Court. The Church wished to convert the Jews from their faith to Orthodoxy while the Court dealt with the problem in a secular and generally obnoxious manner. Nicholas I amalgamated the two by compelling Jewish youths to enter the army at the age of twelve for a period of twenty-five years, which gave them every chance of tottering into civilian life at the age of thirty-seven as good, battered Christians.

The see-saw movement of legislation governing the treatment of Jews demonstrated the continual emergence and suppression of a guilty conscience on the part of the Russians. Whereas decrees by Alexander II opened up higher learning to the Jews, these were contradicted by the bestial pogroms under Alexander III. Restrictive legislation with occasional discreet concessions, such as a quota of Jewish students in secondary and primary schools as opposed to a ban, continued until 1917.

Then, as though this continuing anomaly had finally eaten into the public sensibility, all special regulations for Jews were abolished on 11 March, which also happened to be the first day of the Passover that year.

It must be said that despite, and perhaps even to a certain extent because of, the intransigence shown by the Church and the autocracy towards Jews, the Russian intelligentsia was as free from the blight of anti-semitism as it is today.

In the annals of the Communist Party, Jewish names occur with astonishing regularity. As long ago as 1883, the *quadrum virate* which created the first Russian Marxist group was composed of Plekhanov, Vera Zazulich, both Russian revolutionaries, Akselrod and Lev Deutsch. Among the most influential early Bolshevik leaders Lenin (Ulyanov) was Russian, Dzugaskvili was Georgian, and Trotsky (Bronstein), Kamenev (Rosenfeldt) and Zinoviev (Radomyslsky) were Jewish.

In 1930, Litvinov (Wallach) took over the Foreign Ministry from Chicherin, and at one time the ambassadors in London, Paris and Washington were all Jewish.

Lenin's study in the Kremlin

If today there are demonstrations in the United States and elsewhere in support of Soviet Jewry, it is largely because of the creation of the State of Israel, and the reluctance of the Soviet government to allow an exodus in the direction of a National Home to the creation of which it was among the first to subscribe. This is a subject which is delicate, and which must therefore be discussed objectively and unemotionally. It is undeniable that among the gifts displayed by Jews are not only those of introspective, balanced wisdom, but also those of extremism and imbalance. Prophets invariably have a bit of both. Jews have been both stubborn in the insistence of their right to worship and, at times, violent in their abrogation of all mysticism. They have brought forth both Jesus Christ and Karl Marx, and have, in most cases, indulged in the final luxury of following neither, while waiting for a third.

Not all Soviet Jews yearn to go to Israel. Some of them leave, but go to the United States, where they sometimes feel lost in a society so free as to seem to their directed senses to have no moral purpose. Some do go to Israel, and feel the friction of a tiny melting-pot. Others stay in the Soviet Union, fully integrated in that system, for better or for worse. They regard Zionism as a natural enemy of Socialism, a militant

Lenin's funeral. His Mausoleum was to become a national shrine and a place of pilgrimage.

recreation of Biblical dreams, the realization of which will, by definition, bring the perpetrators into conflict with their neighbours.

The Jews, like the Russians, gravitate naturally into communes. Because of historical pressures, the community feeling is very strong. And despite all the fears and hostility lavished on it, the word Communism derives from this simple source. Collective farm may be a pejorative phrase in some places, whereas *kibbutz* captures all the glamour of a struggle against an ungrateful soil, but basically the two concepts are identical. The Jews, for so long the tragic victims of circumstances, are now for the first time in a position of authority over others, and perhaps with their natural sensitivity, at least some of them may realize that their experiences on the Left Bank are not much more praiseworthy than the ugly manners of the Tsar in a period of far less general enlightenment. The existence of second-class citizens, be they Jews, Arabs, Africans, is always a disgrace, and worthy of unqualified condemnation.

Naturally the Jews have the complex of exclusivity, germane to numerically small peoples. The physical difference between a ghetto and a club is that you cannot get out of the one at night and you cannot get into the other during the day, but what you make of this difference is dependent on the individual attitude. Arrogance can easily translate the fact that you are locked in into the fact that others are locked out, and the unsuspecting tourist may well sense a feeling of vengeance in Israel as he is compelled to live according to the precepts of Jewish law whatever his religion.

Russia has complexes which are the consequences of size: a certain negligence in the niceties of social intercourse; a tendency to disregard time; a stand-offishness which is resignation to the inevitability of boredom rather than pride. But these obvious differences apart, the two peoples have had a lasting affect on each other, both in manner and in matter. At least, with all the errors of the past, and accusations of the present, they have never had a chance of becoming indifferent to one another.

Socialism in One Country

Russia needed every friend she could find. She made peace with the new republican Turkey under Mustafa Kemal in 1921. This was the end of a traditional enmity, and facilitated the reoccupation of Armenia, Georgia, and Azerbaijan, which became Soviet republics, as did the Ukraine. Treaties were also concluded with Afghanistan, Iran and Outer Mongolia, which passed out of the Chinese area of influence, and into the Soviet orbit.

China herself was just waking after centuries of self-sufficiency. Sun Yat Sen had just made China conscious of her nationhood, and an automatic sympathy sprang up between the two nations, especially since the Soviets abrogated the treaty between China and Imperial Russia as being inequitable. The Chinese Eastern Railroad, formerly under Tsarist control, was now under joint Chinese and Soviet management. Outstanding young Chinese came to complete their studies in the Soviet Union, including Chiang Kai Shek. A Russian military mission was at hand to train the Chinese in the refinements of modern warfare.

In the West, Russia and Germany surprised and disturbed the European powers by signing a treaty at Rapallo on 16 April 1922 which declared all war claims to be invalid, and promised closer economic and political relations. Although the United States, under Herbert Hoover, had answered the impassioned plea for aid from Maxim Gorky, the writer, by organizing famine relief on a large scale after the catastrophic harvest of 1921, there could be no question yet of American recognition of the Soviet Union. America has always needed a long time to recover from the shock of any revolution but her own, as evidence the long time it took for her to recognize that great changes had taken place on the Chinese mainland after the Second World War, and that the island of Formosa, or Taiwan, could hardly be considered as a legitimate alter ego for the hundred million souls on the mainland. The Russian revolution was no exception to this rule of weighing up all the evidence before a definite commitment could be made. Britain, France and Italy found it expedient to recognize the Soviet government in 1924. The United States delayed its decision until 17 November 1933, and then did so only because of Hitler's accession to power in Germany!

Within Russia, Lenin's death had created a dangerous situation. No sooner were the embalmed remains of the father of the revolution safely in the mausoleum on the Kremlin's outer wall, than the struggle for power was under way. The leadership was taken over by a triumvirate, composed of Kamenev, leader of the Moscow Party organization, Zinoviev, leader of the Leningrad Party organization, and Stalin, Secretary General of the Party.

Maxim Gorky (1868–1936).

The New Economic Policy had been such a success that whereas in 1921 imports had exceeded exports by over one hundred per cent, by 1924 imports were only two-thirds of exports. Naturally the chance it gave middle-men to prosper caused increased industrial production but it also created conditions which brought frowns to the faces of the purists. Statistics show that gambling casinos, cabarets, restaurants and other places of amusement paid ten million roubles in taxes into the coffers of the municipality of Moscow for the year 1923 alone. The rapid recovery of Russian agriculture and industry began to attract short-term foreign capital once again, but the old believers of the Bolshevik movement began to cry heresy as the old believers of the Orthodox Church had cried in the past. Now, however, the phantom of the anti-Christ had been superseded by that of the counter-revolutionary, a *nouveau-riche* bourgeois profiting by a laxity in dogma to line his own pocket.

The result of this was the formation of the Comintern, or Communist International, devoted to world revolution by propaganda, espionage, and fomentation of revolt. This organization, which embalmed Lenin's dream as effectively as the dreamer, caused practically all the achievements of skilled Russian diplomacy to be nullified. Its special distinction was that it embraced all Communist parties as ostensibly equal partners, so that the possibilities of subversion were in the hands of Communist 'cells' in various parts of the world, including the colonies of great powers. Quite obviously the existence of such an apparatus inhibited the credibility of Russian ambassadors, who were believed to be mere façades before this sinister contagion.

In 1923, Lord Curzon, the British Foreign Secretary, was constrained to make a protest of unusual virulence about Russian propaganda in Britain and her colonies. Four years later, the British police raided the headquarters of Arcos, the Soviet Trade delegation in London, confiscating documents the contents of which were never revealed, but which were evidently of such a combustible nature as to justify a breaking off of diplomatic relations by both Britain and Canada.

In the Far East, things were no better. Despite the patching up of old quarrels, the Chinese police raided the Soviet Embassy in Peking, with the consequence that Chiang Kai Shek got rid of all Communists in the armed forces, and an actual Communist rising in Canton was forcibly suppressed. Russia was once again betrayed by her own brand of puritanism.

A reflection of this disharmony was apparent in the inner struggles of the Party. In the final shake-up there were those of moderate and pragmatic tendency like Bukharin, Rykov and Tomsky, who believed that the virtues of the New Economic Policy outweighed its vices, and that a degree of incentive must be preserved. Opposed to them were Zinoviev, now head of the Comintern, Kamenev, and Trotsky, the firebrand

Stalin, standing beside Lenin's tomb in Red Square, reviews a parade in 1926, to commemorate the October Revolution of 1917.

orator, believers in the permanency of revolution, and rapid industrialization. And there was Stalin.

Stalin bided his time, and used his power as Secretary General of the Party judiciously. Curiously enough, it was the bumper crop of 1926 which precipitated the violent argument that rich peasants were making profits too great to be compatible with Party doctrine. They were becoming the wealthy rustic counterparts to the urban parasites who patronized the gambling halls and the cafés of Moscow. Matters became so heated that Trotsky and Zinoviev were expelled from the Party. Kamenev was downgraded to Soviet Ambassador to Italy. Once this was accomplished, Stalin turned on his allies within the Party, and coolly adopted the very policies for which Trotsky and his accomplices had been punished.

In case it be thought that politics in the Stalinist era was relatively cut and dried, merely a two-dimensional conflict between good guys and bad guys seen through the Communist prism, it is as well for a moment to dwell on the Agatha Christie-like destinies of the men who led the government of this massive nation after Lenin's death.

Trotsky was expelled from the Party in 1927, and exiled to Alma-Ata, in the far republic of Kazakhstan. Here he lived, dedicated to polemical

Caricature of Leon Trotsky

writing until his final banishment for life in 1929. He eventually settled in Mexico but was murdered in 1940 by a young Frenchman, believed to have been an agent of the Soviet government. Two married daughters and a son disappeared in Russia. The remaining son was murdered in France, all before their father's death.

Zinoviev was expelled at the same time as Trotsky, but was taken back into the Party on recantation of his heresies in 1928. In 1932, however, he was expelled again. In 1933, he was taken back again. After the murder of Kirov, a powerful Stalinist, in 1935, so close to the dictator as to inspire jealousy not only in others, but in Stalin himself, Zinoviev was sentenced to ten years in prison for 'Moral Complicity' in the murder. He only served one year of his sentence, however, because in 1936 he was re-tried and executed.

Kamenev, as we have noted, was Ambassador to Italy from 1926 to 1927. Like the other two, he was expelled from the Party in 1927, and like Zinoviev, reaccepted in 1928, re-expelled in 1932, re-reaccepted in 1933. After Kirov's murder, he was sentenced to five years for the same mysterious 'Moral Complicity', but he too was re-tried in 1936, and executed.

And what of the other three, who had supported Stalin's attack on Trotsky?

Stalin turned on them as soon as Trotsky and his colleagues had been expelled from the Party, accusing them of 'rightist deviation'.

Rykov was dismissed until his recantation in 1931, and even after suffering humiliation and shame at the Seventeenth Congress, he acted out his contrition so well that he was put forward as a candidate member of the Central Committee of the Bolshevik Party. A vain hope, for in 1938 he was tried for treason and executed.

Bukharin, who was Stalin's chief ally against Trotsky, suddenly fell from favour, being described as a falsifier of the Marxist creed, and was

Trotsky and his family in exile

Stalin and friends at a picnic in 1930

stripped of all his official functions. Nonetheless, he later became editor of *Izvestia*, the official government newspaper, but in 1937 he was expelled from the Party on the extraordinary charge of being a Trotskyist! The next year he was found guilty of treason, and executed.

And what of Tomsky? In 1936, he merely committed suicide, the lucky fellow.

Of all the leading figures of the post-Lenin period, only one died in his bed. Stalin.

It is a curious European phenomenon that on three occasions, important nations have fallen victim to the dictatorship of foreigners, always coming from the south, and dominating more industrious peoples to the north. Napoleon began the trend when, as a Corsican, he waited for the bright flame of revolution to burn itself out, and then deflected the new spirit to serve his particular gifts. Stalin, from Georgia, had the mind of a tycoon, always one step ahead of the fiery Jewish intellectuals, with their grasp of abstractions, and of the Russians, who merely wished that things that were going well would go better. He had a cynical disregard for theory, although he paid it lipservice when necessary. Had he lived in America, he would certainly have worked

174

himself into a position of control in a large corporation, or rather, the largest corporation, and would have got his way by killing hardly anybody. He was more of a godfather figure than a father figure, and finally the only one of the three to know real, if horrible, success.

Hitler, the third of the trinity, from Austria, was too shrill in his courtship of destiny, and never gave himself a chance to rise to any kind of heights as a Prince of Darkness. He lacked Napoleon's style and impertinence, and Stalin's smiling detachment. He merely looked to the heavens in plebeian exasperation, inventing intuitions when none were forthcoming, and dragged half the world with him in an orgy of death and destruction.

None of the three did their neighbours much good, but Stalin was certainly the most casual in his betrayals, the most secret in his fears, and the most soft-spoken in his outbursts. As all such men must, he had a low opinion of his fellows, and exploited their weaknesses more thoroughly than their strengths. On Russia, he had the effect of a Tartar army, but he was more demanding in the collection of the tributes due to him.

A notorious series of Five-Year Plans were his official legacy, which projected the future progress of the nation in Draconian terms. Nothing was left to chance. The individuals who had operated so successfully

Stalin reading on his boat

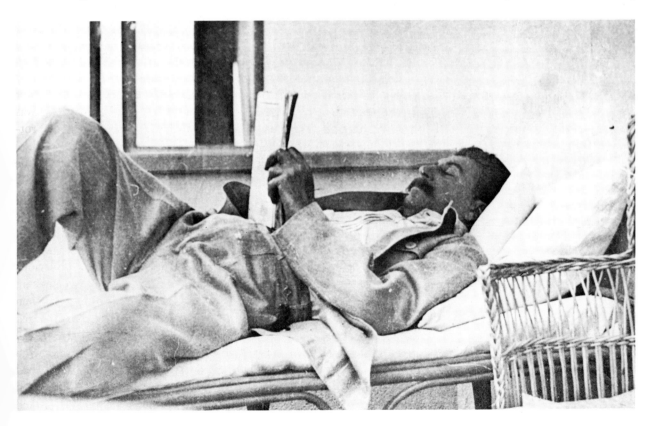

under the New Economic Policy were snuffed out of existence, as were the richer peasants, by prohibitive taxation. Everything and everyone was collectivized, and the greatest emphasis of all was on heavy industry, without which a modern nation could not make provision for its own defence or even independence.

In the course of this relentless uniformity, nothing was spared to make the country efficient, and drab. The arts, which had flourished in reckless profusion at the moment of revolution, were mobilized and regimented into a devitalized sameness. The *avant-garde*, such as Malevich, Vladimir Tatlin, and Alexandra Ekster in the graphic arts, Meyerhold in the theatre, Mayakovsky, Blok, and Yesenin in poetry, Eisenstein and Pudovkin in the cinema, could no longer operate, or had died. The survivors were subjected to endless proscriptions by obtuse officials, who behaved as though it were possible to make five-year plans for the spirit as well as for the body. A ridiculous style of Socialist realism was devised for the visual arts, in which painters were expected to imitate photography in the description of various aspects of heroism, or to illustrate the vileness of the opposition. The movies were emasculated after their brilliant beginnings, and composers were continually chided for traces of modernity in their scoring and symptoms of pessimism in their melodies. The function of the arts in society was negated, and they were treated as just another branch of industry. The strictures of men like Zhdanov and other arbiters of public taste rank high in the records of human insensitivity and brutal stupidity.

Although industry developed at a cracking pace, the collectivization of agriculture, and the immense influx of people from the country into towns prompted the first signs of a food crisis which has survived to this day.

In 1928, nearly all peasants were individual farmers on small-holdings. State Farms and Collective Farms represented under 3 per cent of Russian agriculture. By 1934, State and Collective Farms accounted for $86\frac{1}{2}$ per cent, with individual holdings reduced to $13\frac{1}{2}$ per cent.

With the coming of the second Five-Year Plan there was no alleviation of the prevalent sameness, although the differences in salaries between skilled and unskilled workers became far more marked, as did the differences between the upper bureaucracy and the lower, and the lower and the worker. A new hierarchy was rapidly developing, and in a way, a new aristocracy of the left with, however, the important proviso that even if nepotism and influence played a part, as it must in all large societies, this aristocracy was not based on heredity of any sort, but was purely a matter of merit, and acceptance of the prevalent grey discipline.

There were certain changes of attitude, too, which came with the undoubted stabilization of the State, and a feeling of growing power. The past was examined with greater thoroughness. Tsarism was no longer summarily dismissed as having been a bad thing. Even men

A still from the film, *Ivan the Terrible*, made by Sergei Eisenstein in 1945, where the character of Ivan was reassessed in the light of contemporary values.

like Ivan the Terrible were re-examined, and the positive contributions of his reign to the greatness of the nation highlighted, a pastime which was curiously apt during the hegemony of Stalin. Although 'bourgeois' was still the dirtiest of words, the Russia of Stalin became distinctly bourgeois in character, which is one of the hallmarks of success and affluence. Domestic life gravitated around potted palms and table-runners, in the shadow of neo-gothic skyscrapers. And divorce, once so easy in the bohemian atmosphere of the early revolutionary days, was now made extremely difficult, and abortion, that final liberation of the woman from the doctrine of religion, was forbidden altogether.

Stalin, perhaps partly because he was a foreigner, or at least, a foreigner to the traditions of Russia, was never an internationalist. He had no faith in the abstractions of world revolution while there were unsolved questions in the only revolution over which he had control, the Russian one. In fact, he postulated his view in the statement,

'Socialism in One Country', as early as 1924. In his view, Socialism had to be constructed in Russia, without reference to potential Communist uprisings in other countries. This objectivity was at the base of his quarrel with the firebrands like Trotsky.

The now familiar Soviet plea for disarmament began back in 1922, when the government sought an arms limitation agreement with its neighbours, Poland, Finland, Estonia, Latvia and Lithuania. In 1927, at a conference in Geneva, the Soviet delegate proposed a progressive diminution of land, sea and air forces, to be initiated forthwith. The proposal was rejected by the European powers.

This cold shoulder, and other signs of hostility, drove the Soviet government into a rapprochement with Germany. When Germany made proposals for disarmament, she was supported by the Soviet Union.

When Hitler acceded to power in 1933, the whole pattern of European alliances changed. The basis of his platform was a violent anti-communism, which had found favour with the captains of industry who had facilitated his rise to the Chancellorship, and a repudiation of the Treaty of Versailles, which had imposed humiliating conditions on Germany. Litvinov, the Soviet Foreign Commissar, was not slow to take the hint, and formulated for the first time the idea of collective security, in the conviction that peace was indivisible. 1934, the year that Germany walked out of the League of Nations, Russia walked in.

There had been alliances galore throughout the ages, but it was only when practically every large nation, and most small ones, were actively engaged in the interdependent political life of a continent diminished by the speed of communication, that the idea of collective security could be mooted. That the idea emanated from Russia is to her credit, but it also meant that others had misgivings. Many were those in important positions, especially in England, who saw in Hitler and Mussolini the welcome symptoms of efficiency, without understanding that this efficiency would later be applied to warfare. The modernity of auto-bahns and the apparent investment of the Italian State Railways with quite un-Latin qualities bamboozled some sleepy members of the British establishment into a kind of gentle jealousy.

With France, always a land of radical rhetoric accompanied more often than not by quite conservative actions, the Russians were more successful, at least for a time. The Comintern, always seen as the power behind the throne by its clarion calls for insurrection and continuous mischief in more subtle ways, abruptly changed its policy, embracing the fellow traveller instead of despising him, and calling for a union of all against the expansionist and anti-semitic platform of the Nazis. This intelligent change of emphasis enabled a pact of mutual assistance to be concluded with France, and in 1936, the French *Front-Populaire* government of Leon Blum, included Communist ministers in the cabinet for the first time. A pact of mutual assistance was also concluded with Czechoslovakia, but with the rider that it would only be operative if the French were also involved militarily. Non-aggression agreements were concluded with the immediate neighbours of the Soviet Union, Romania, Poland, Lithuania, Latvia, Estonia and Finland.

The Japanese invasion of China in 1937 was the origin of a Sino-Soviet Treaty, and the Russians began supplying arms and technical advisers to the armies of Chiang Kai Shek.

The outbreak of the Spanish Civil War, one of the most important events of the century in retrospect, and to a far-sighted few at the time, put all these agreements to the test. In March 1936, the insurrection of

V. M. Molotov.

General Franco against the legitimate government of the Spanish Republic began, and quickly acquired the full support of German and Italian armies and air forces, who used the occasion to practise their techniques of warfare against Spanish towns and Spanish people. Russia intervened on the side of legitimacy with aircraft, arms, and advisers, but the countries were far away from each other geographically. Spanish ministers and French intellectuals appealed for French intervention, but the *Front-Populaire*, under intense pressure from Britain, remained neutral and inactive, merely organizing facilities for refugees. By her firm action, Britain at that moment, guaranteed the outbreak of the Second World War, which had, in fact, already begun, while Lenin's misgivings about leftwing sympathisers was amply justified. In the final analysis, coalitions of the left surrounded the communists with a woolly cloud of commitment, which evaporated at the first breath of cold wind.

Shortly after the collapse of the democratically elected Spanish government before the forces of fascism, the ideas of collective security were put to another test. Germany decided to reclaim her Sudeten minorities in Czechoslovakia. War was avoided for the time being by a degrading encounter between Hitler, Mussolini, Chamberlain and

Molotov watched by Stalin signing the ten-year non-aggression pact with Germany in 1939.

Daladier in Munich to which the Russians were not invited, despite their treaty with Czechoslovakia. The Czechs were abandoned in the most cowardly fashion since, according to Neville Chamberlain, it was a 'distant land of which we know little'. Geography was certainly not Mr Chamberlain's forte. On a later occasion, when it was announced that German troops had taken Narvik, in the north of Norway, in one of their lightning advances, he announced to the House of Commons that there must have been an error in transmission, and the telegram should have read Larvik, close to Oslo. It is only a shoddy workman who blames his telegrams.

These disappointments were enough to change the orientation of Soviet Foreign policy once again. Litvinov, the reasonable, the hopeful idealist was replaced by Molotov, a man who had chosen his *nom-de-guerre*, as had Stalin. Stalin suggests steel, while Molot means hammer. Molotov, whose real name was Scriabin, made his intentions abundantly clear. With his button nose, and his glinting *pince-nez* under the huge dome of his forehead, he provided a fitting figurehead for the ship of state as it changed direction in a rough sea.

There was an outcry of outraged morality from the West when Communist Russia and Nazi Germany signed a non-aggression pact on 23 August 1939. It bore every sign of a pragmatic accommodation. The act was admittedly cold-blooded and calculating, and at the expense of Poland, the traditional buffer of the West. Poland's misfortune, however, was that she was not only a buffer of the West, but also, in modern history, a buffer of the East. The Russians were reacting to the period of optimism, in which their hand was extended and only grudgingly accepted, or refused altogether. She has always been as sensitive to the situation on her borders as Britain has been to her status at sea, and enough was enough.

The return of Chamberlain to Britain brandishing, as he stepped from his aircraft, a promissory note from Hitler, 'I have here a piece of paper!', applauded by most of a nation, was no less an act of perfidy than the Russo-German pact, and yet the hands which clapped the one were thrown up in horror at the other.

When Germany, liberated from the threat of a major war on two fronts as in 1914, attacked Poland on 1 September, Britain and France did the honourable thing at last by declaring war on Germany on 3 September. The Russians, liberated from their treaty obligations to the West, entered Poland on 17 September, and, by evident pre-arrangement, occupied their half. While they were about it, they waited briefly until the Germans were busy in the West, and then re-annexed the Baltic States and took back Bessarabia and Northern Bukovina from Romania. They were, in a sense, taking their revenge not merely on the Treaty of Brest Litovsk in 1917, but on those who had taken advantage of their weakness then by annexing pieces of the Russian Empire at that

Chamberlain returns to Britain after his
meeting with Hitler in Munich.

time. It will be remembered, for instance, that the reconstituted Poland
contained four million ethnic Russians.

But certainly the principal reason for their temporary complicity
with the Germans was to enlarge as far as possible the buffer between
themselves and their potential and undoubted enemy. To suggest, as is
fashionable, that the eventual German aggression on the Soviet Union
took Stalin by surprise is to invest him with naivety, which is tantamount
to attributing the quality of grace to Hitler. No, the Russians have
always made a military virtue of space, which is natural, since they were

born with it. Once again, as natural as for the British to think in terms of water. With the increasing speed of modern warfare, space had become somewhat devalued, but was still of paramount importance to a land with enormous frontiers to protect. An enemy would be compelled to show his hand on acquired soil before he could possibly reach Russian territory. To this end, in November, 1939, the Soviet armies attacked Finland, despite their non-aggression treaty, in order to push the border further away from Leningrad and to acquire sites for naval bases. Once again, the West was horrified and Finland became as eloquent a symbol of gallant integrity as Belgium had been twenty-five years before.

What is generally attributed in the West to Russian aggression is invariably defensive by nature. The thinking is entirely of protection, of cover. Russia has, in fact, never fought an aggressive war in Europe on her own account, nor is she mentally constituted for such an adventure. Even on the eve of the Crimean war, she obeyed the rules of the shoddy game. Her opponents didn't.

CHAPTER FIFTEEN

The Struggle against Fascism

At the time of the McCarthy hearings in America, set up to investigate alleged communist infiltration into the American armed forces, a phrase was coined which was quite horrid in its implications. It was 'Premature Anti-Fascist', and it referred to those who saw the menace of Hitler's Germany with greater alacrity than was generally fashionable, and who reacted accordingly. Typical of those guilty of this particular fault were the romantic fellows who went off to fight in the Lincoln Brigade in Spain. It is indicative that this heartbreaking event, the simple theme, upon which variations have been played ever since with ever larger and more deafening orchestras, also inspired poets of other lands, poets who would be soldiers as well as soldiers who saw themselves as poets.

Malraux, Hemingway, Lorca were there. MacNeice and many others wrote about it. Mao Tse Tung, Attlee, Marshal Madinovsky put in appearances. Tito worked in the recruiting office in Paris. It was the dress rehearsal for what was to follow, and the most venerable of the British spies were recruited by the Soviet Union.

Hard as it may be to understand how intelligent men can be lured into the furtive world of espionage by foreign powers, this phenomenon cannot be judged today without a modicum of compassion and of decency. Anyone alive and aware at that time can never forget the sickening frustration felt by some people in Britain at the aura of somnolence which radiated from high quarters; politicians who seemed serenely unaware of Hitler's elaborate preparations for war. There was no secret about this. The Rhineland was reoccupied by the Germans, the military restrictions of the Versailles Treaty repudiated, there was marching and countermarching and all the symptoms of militancy; incentives for fecundity in women such as *Mütterchenringe*, rings of honour with interchangeable numerals at their centre to record increase in the family, gifts to the serried ranks of the Third Reich. Then the disgusting racial theories were promulgated, windows of shops owned by Jews were smashed and their contents looted with official sanction, the first concentration camps were built, although they still had a way to go before they attained their eventual refinement.

The Italians began to see themselves as not only the spiritual but the actual inheritors of ancient Rome. The pomp was there, all that was now needed was the circumstances. They invaded Ethiopia, one of the only bits of Africa still available for colonial adventure. They had tried before, in less energetic times, and been annihilated at Adona, towards the end of the nineteenth century. Now they thirsted for revenge, but it was only with enormous difficulty that this thirst was slaked.

Hitler with Field Marshal Goering passes standards carrying the names of fallen German airmen of the Condor Legion who fought in Spain: the flamboyance of Fascism which so easily attracts the simple-minded.

Not long afterwards, they set a precedent in carrying aggression back to Europe again by annexing Albania, after a brief conflict which was never conclusive. Albanian warriors returned to their mountain fortresses as the Yugoslavs were to do subsequently. With all this evidence, the British government still put on the brave face of indifference. It was even deaf to the entreaties of certain German generals to stand firm against a machine which was as yet far from ready. The Munich Agreement went through despite all opposition, refining the process of what became known as 'appeasement', and which had started when there was no reaction to the *fait-accompli* of the Rhineland occupation, and continued with the miserable Hoare-Laval plan to accommodate the criminal without too great a loss to the victim during the Ethiopian war.

The excuse given for the Munich Pact subsequently was that it gave Britain and France time to prepare. Prepare for what? Dunkirk and the fall of France?

Up to the rape of Czechoslovakia, the Soviet Union was the one major power which seemed to be aware of the inevitability of conflict, and which expressed ideas at worst less selfish, at best more human than those of Germany and Italy. There is a recurrent cliché among cosy people that Fascism and Communism are identical. Fascism is a form of militant nostalgia, with more of a mystique than a platform. In the hands of Central or South American generals, there is not usually the mental capacity for a platform, but plenty of noisy rhetoric at the disposal of a simple mystique. Hitler had found his inspiration in Wagnerian music and the attendant German legends; Mussolini reconstructed the triumphal arches for the return of victorious warriors; the Japanese turned for inspiration to the exploits of the Samurai now at the controls of flimsy aircraft, in quest of honourable death.

Fascism is invariably simple-minded, based on the premise that discipline is the freedom of the ignorant. There are very few theories attached to it in its usual form. It is basically flamboyant, grandiloquent and the friend and ally of large financial interests, who have as much to gain from discipline as the military leader with an eye for patterns on the parade grounds. It inspires confidence in the status quo because it 'works', and its aggressions stimulate the economy.

Communism is far more complicated, a religion for intellectuals. It is founded on universal, as opposed to particular, ideals. It is obsessed with morality. The Constitution of the Soviet Union is a fine document with an understandably different emphasis from its celebrated American counterpart. The fundamental rights of the individual are related to duty towards the state and not as a protection from the state. In the US Constitution, the state is, by implication, a necessary evil: in the Soviet Constitution, it is a necessary good.

Opinions vary as to the relative excellences of the two very different ways of looking at the world and of assessing the importance of the

individual in them. Yet it is undeniable that there was always enough on the face of Communism to attract the intellectual during those exasperating pre-war years, and it was then, in the universities, that the young men who eventually became spies were recruited. Today they are attacked in the media as men who betrayed their country to an enemy. This is, of course, an injustice of reprehensible facility.

When Hitler attacked Russia on 22 June 1941, he did one important thing which is rarely mentioned. He put an end to the possibilities of 'premature anti-fascism'. The democracies and the Soviet Union were flung into an alliance which was always distinctly uneasy, and only made possible by Hitler's insane views. In those days, the spies were doing whatever work they did in favour of a friendly power, but that is carefully never mentioned, since the friendship was merely technical. And then, no one has ever been punished for being a 'premature anti-communist'. There has never been any need.

The war in the East began with huge convulsions in the field. As always when Russia was attacked, there was a general feeling that the aggressors would probably win. It had happened in 1812, and in 1914, and again at the time of the Allied interventions in 1918. Russian arms were not trusted to do the job. There was much talk of 'General Winter', as though hellish conditions alone would stop the clever Germans, who must have known what they were doing, otherwise they would never have embarked on such an adventure. Stalin's paranoid elimination of military leaders such as General Tukhachevsky in 1937 had skimmed the cream from the army. The release of Marshal Rokossovsky from confinement to take over a high command seemed to confirm the rumours of rottenness. Everything appeared to be as wayward and as wild as in the days of Ivan the Terrible – three fronts of the usual enormous lengths under the commands of an unknown, the egg-headed Marshal Timoshenko, a veteran, Voroshilov, then aged sixty, a personal friend of Stalin, and a cavalryman hero of the Civil War, Budyonny, who sported enormous whiskers and was reputed to carry the dowry of an unmarried daughter with him whever he went, in case he met an eligible young man.

Stalin justified the German-Soviet pact in a speech of 3 July as a necessary act which had given Russia time to prepare. This was for internal consumption, and its purpose was obviously to give an explanation to the inconsistency of Soviet foreign policy to a public accustomed to regard the Nazis as anathema. Actually, the indecisions of the West had given Russia no alternative to a temporary accommodation with the Germans if they held out any hopes for their arms to prevail. In this connection, Stalin also called for a policy of scorched-earth just as Alexander I had done when Napoleon attacked almost a hundred and thirty years before. It was evident from the start that the Germans could not be prevented from advancing initially.

Lenin: an idealized visionary

They took Kiev on 19 September. Kharkov followed on 24 October, and the Crimea was occupied, although Sebastopol only fell on 2 July 1942. The Russian losses in these initial advances were enormous. Over two million soldiers were taken prisoner, and there was a commensurate loss in equipment. Leningrad was more or less surrounded, and the Germans stood within thirty kilometres of Moscow. The capital was moved to Kuibyshev, southeast of Moscow. Many industries necessary for the war effort were moved bodily to the Ural mountains and other locations in the hinterland.

When 'General Winter' finally intervened, the Germans were in possession of vast territories, but had not succeeded in striking a blow which was in any way decisive. Also the initial Soviet commanders had been relegated to other functions, and new leaders began to emerge, formed by experience of battle and the tough school of exigency. Among them was Zhukov, who mounted the first successful counter-attack against the Germans. It had no great strategic importance, but it showed that there was still a sting in the Russian armoury, and that initiatives could be, and would be taken.

After the thaw of 1942, the Germans made their greatest effort, with all the delusions of finality. It aimed at the south, at oil and wheat. Rostov fell, the Don was crossed, the Caucasus was overrun. By

The Germans raise the flag over Sebastopol on 2 July 1942

Soviet troops in Stalingrad, November 1942

August, the Germans were at the gates of Stalingrad on the Volga. The name of the city seemed to hypnotize Hitler, and he committed his troops as though its capture could be decisive and indeed the battle proved a dramatic turning point in his fortunes.

As they had done in the past so often as to become a tradition, the Russians managed to temporize with one hand while training new armies and manufacturing new arms with the other. This time, they did not fall into the Tsarist trap of neglecting the tools and leaving their men practically defenceless. Neither did they launch their counter-attack before they were ready. The battle for Stalingrad was one of ferocious attrition, Hitler like a deranged gambler committing all his remaining capital to the same losing chip, the Russians riding the storm, giving way inch by inch until the new, fresh armies were ready. For three months the awful carnage lasted, until 'General Winter' obligingly intervened again. On 19 November, the Russians launched a sudden counter-attack in the form of weighty pincers, supported by an immense tangle of artillery and katyusha rockets, and four days later, when the blades of the pincers met on the snow behind the German 6th Army, 200,000 shattered troops were isolated from the divisions on their flanks. The Germans launched ferocious assaults to relieve the embattled army of General van Paulus, but the Russians held firm, and on the last day of January the German commander, afflicted with a nervous twitching of the eye, surrendered. His consolation was to be promoted to the rank of Field Marshal by Hitler.

On 2 February 1943, the German
Sixth Army surrendered at Stalingrad,
cut off from the main German southern
front by Russian counter-offensive
moves. It was an appalling blow to the
German Army and a turning point
in the war.

A satirical cartoon shows Hitler and
Mussolini sheltering under an umbrella
from the Allied storm.

By midsummer of 1943, the tortoise had caught and passed the
wounded hare. Hitler committed his dishevelled troops to a final
offensive, which broke itself against the new Soviet armies under
Zhukov, Koniev, Rokossovsky and Meretskov. In the north, Smolensk
fell. In the south, Kiev. Every day, the news summaries on the Russian
radio announced the fall of towns and cities to the thunder of guns.

By the middle of 1944, the Red Army had recaptured all the territory
it had lost and crossed into the lands occupied by the enemy. At the
same time, the Allies disembarked in Normandy.

The precipitate advance took the Russians to the Vistula, to the out-
skirts of Warsaw. The Polish Resistance Army under General Bor-
Komorowski, rose and showed its hand, under the impression that the
Russians were about to cross the river. The fact that the Russians did

not, and that the uprising was suppressed with the utmost brutality by the Germans, who destroyed the city under express orders from the enraged Hitler, has always been attributed by Western historians to the vindictive malevolence of Stalin. Since General Bor-Komorowski owed his allegiance to the Polish Government in exile, it is all too easy to lend credence to this version of the truth especially since the Soviets refused permission for Allied planes to land behind the Russian lines after they had dropped supplies to the heroic Poles. However, Marshal Zhukov in his memoirs reports a furious argument between himself and Stalin, during which the latter was categorical about the necessity to press on to Berlin without delay. It was Zhukov who, for purely military and logistical reasons, insisted that the advance guard simply could not run so far ahead of its support troops and supplies without courting disaster. It needed, he said, a regrouping on the defensible line of the Vistula, the last major river before Berlin apart from the Oder, and that a halt must be called if the final blow was to be telling, and Soviet superiority in men and equipment was to be deployed without unnecessary risk. After a bitter row, with biting sarcasm on one side and soldierly bluntness on the other, Stalin smilingly gave in to a superior technical knowledge, and the Russian drive was halted. By implication,

Russian troops in a ruined Berlin

Churchill, Roosevelt and Stalin at the Yalta Conference in 1945

Zhukov maintains that the tragedy of Warsaw was the fault of Polish impatience, and not of Russian duplicity.

This is a typical example of the difficulty in balancing overprotected Soviet history, with its careful Marxist slant, with the prejudices of the West, which are, on the whole, no less tendentious, and no more reliable. The events of Yalta and even the Helsinki Conference are remembered differently on both sides, with divergent terms of reference, and even incompatible vocabularies.

Not only is there a lack of understanding between Soviet Russia and the West but worse, a lack of *a wish* to understand.

CHAPTER SIXTEEN

Communism at Work

Had Russia been a benevolent democracy, with a less predictable posture owing to the fluctuations of a multi-party system, there is little reason to doubt that precisely the same confrontation with the United States would exist as it does today, with perhaps slightly less emphasis on human rights, and a consequent diminution in their attendant hypocrisies.

There was a hope latent in Western minds that Communist Russia and Nazi Germany would somehow cancel each other out, and that, at worst, the destruction of one would so enfeeble the other that the victorious Western democracies could easily re-educate a battered Europe in the virtues of parliamentary democracy. Contrary to all reasonable expectation, the very opposite occurred.

As the war neared its end, and Nazi Germany sank slowly to its knees, the Soviet armies were bloodied, but rampant, stronger than ever despite terrible losses, and the Teheran Conference of 1943 had to find urgent solutions to problems created by the vacuum in the very centre of Europe left after the fall of the German Reich. It needed to be filled in an ordered, and as far as possible, just manner.

It is usual today to blame what is regarded as an Allied surrender to Stalin on the effects of Roosevelt's terminal illness on his judgment. This is to consider the conference as a normal one, without taking into account the very exceptional conditions prevailing both at Teheran and subsequently, at Yalta. First of all there was not much time and agreement was essential. And secondly, at the appalling cost of twenty million casualties, Stalin had won the first conclusive victory in Russian history. Despite American and British aid, and the Allied assault in the West when the tide had already turned against the Nazis, it had to be recognized that the conflict in the East was on an entirely different scale to that in France, Italy, and Africa. Stalin had not lost his enigmatic smile, but it no longer concealed doubts or questions. It was the trade mark of victory and the emblem of self-confidence. Would any other agreement with the Russians have been possible at that moment? Would Roosevelt, even lucid and energetic, have done any better than the white-faced shadow of a man, wrapped in a cape, who stared reality expressionless in the face? Churchill may have been old, but he was not ill, and he did what he could – 'Poland will take two paces to the left'. It may send a chill down the spine of the sensitive, this wholesalers' approach to geopolitical facts, but statesmen cannot be squeamish as they carve up the European cake for the umpteenth time to the pain and confusion of the ingredients. Oh, Stalin could afford to make one or two casual gestures in the direction of free elections here and there, but since he

Stalin, the war leader, kisses the sword of Stalingrad. It was a gift from Churchill (*back to camera*) and the people of Britain and presented in Teheran in December, 1943. Molotov is on Stalin's left.

knew nothing about free elections, and cared less, he really couldn't be expected to be too meticulous in honouring his part of a bargain.

What did concern him, not unnaturally, was security. It was, after all, what had concerned Russia from her untidy and so nearly tragic beginnings and what will always concern her.

It may seem to some that the October Revolution of 1917 had changed the window dressing but very little else, yet that is one of the many penalties of vastness. Smaller countries, anxious about their viability in a troubled world, and more immediately jealous of their national identities, invariably know a great deal about the activities of their neighbours. Frontiers change as time passes and cultural influences flow across them. Not so in Russia. She heard no voices from the next room. Whenever she wished for glimpses of what others were up to, she had to organize great Embassies, as in the days of Ivan the Terrible and Peter the Great, with the specific mandate of looking, listening, and digesting.

Lenin may have travelled, but how could he adapt his findings to Russian conditions? In any case, he was more interested in Marxist theory, as untried in the West as in the East. And those with experience of other lands and other systems were the very class which suffered exile as the least of the discomforts heaped upon it.

Stalin had no experience of foreign countries, and no great desire to acquire such experience. Teheran was selected as a meeting place because he had no wish to travel further from the arena of his triumphs. He himself had suggested Fairbanks in Alaska as a more suitable locale, but was persuaded against it. All of which proves that the horizons of his limited world were the walls of the Kremlin, a fastness within which many of Russia's despotic rulers had nurtured their dreams and felt the fever of paranoia grip them in hermetic isolation. It was a destiny for which a seminary in Georgia was probably not the worst of schools.

In other words, the terms of reference for a renewal of Russia was Russia itself, its personality and history, to the exclusion of any other influence apart from a theoretical work of enormous effectiveness which replaced the Bible in the minds of officialdom if not in the hearts of the entire population.

How could Russia then have changed? Now could the waves on the surface have influenced its undertow, those deep currents of reflexes conditioned by centuries of precarious existence and patient survival? It was, and is, too much to ask.

Stalin, despite all the terrors of his reign, the disappearances and barbarous trials, was associated with the remorseless necessities of victory in battle, and therefore earned his immortality by having been at the right place at the right time. There was no proof, there never is, but it seemed as if no other man could have done the same job with the degree of ruthless resilience or singlemindedness which the successful prosecution of a war on such an inhuman scale demanded. Like other basically repellent but endlessly fascinating figures in the tormented history of Russia, an acceptance of his uncouth and callous character appeared to be a condition of a people's triumph against adversity.

He can never be forgiven for the suffering he caused in thousands of individual cases, but the communal conscience accepted it as an evil which had become necessary once the Nazi invasion had been launched.

There have been endless speculations in our time as to what would happen when this or that outsize figure disappeared. France after de Gaulle, Yugoslavia after Tito, Spain after Franco, China after Mao, were subjects of endless and often quite erroneous conjecture. Owing to the extraordinary diffusion of information, and misinformation, the media had succeeded in making personalities seem indispensable, as though they embodied not only the authority of a nation, but that nation itself. Despite all the Cassandra-like auguries of the experts, very little happened with the passing of any of these men. Other, lesser men

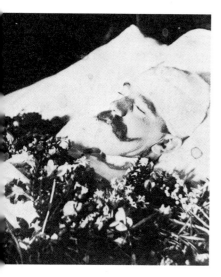

Stalin on his death-bed. At the end he was suspecting even his doctors of trying to murder him and it was not impossible that his fears were justified.

merely went to work as usual, and assumed a certain natural continuity.

The one exception to this was Stalin whose melodramatic end, of a series of massive strokes, was variously reported and interpreted. The sigh of relief could have been recorded seismographically. After a moment of disbelief it was clear that an era really was over.

Ilya Erenburg wrote a novel with a symbolic title, *The Thaw*, and the peppery Nikita Khrushchev summoned up the courage to denounce the more flagrant aspects of the long winter of discontent in a famous speech made in 1956. But once the relief at the lancing of the boil was fact, care was taken to dress the wound, sterilize it from the possibility of Western contagion, and allow the thick skin to grow once more.

The fearful frustrations of the Cold War were over, the litany of vetoes within the United Nations had come to an end, but there was no real change in the character of the confrontation, merely in the manner. There was an avuncular merriment about Khrushchev which came as a distinct relief from the dull façade of Stalin, enlivened only by his feline smile of secret satisfaction. Khrushchev travelled where Stalin had stayed at home. His portly figure was seen garlanded in India and clowning in Hollywood, and examining ears of corn in the Middle West. He went all over the place, to trade wisecracks and peasant saws, but with a moral obligation to teach rather than to learn.

Amazingly, the Americans almost took this tetchy, ebullient figure to their hearts, as though every family had a Khrushchev of its own among its greyer sheep, an explosive elderly relative with a habit of speaking his mind even under unfortunate circumstances, but one whom it was always possible to forgive.

It was this very quality, one of overt humanity, which paradoxically proved his eventual undoing among his own people. Dag Hammarskjöld would show friends the photographs of the famous 'shoe incident' in the United Nations, when Khrushchev beat a rhythm by using a shoe as a drumstick against the desk in order to foment a schoolboyish rebellion. It was an incident remembered when its cause is generally forgotten, and it was carried out with undeniable exuberance. Hammarskjöld was deeply shocked by it, however, and proved by his photographs that Khrushchev was wearing both his own shoes during his jam session, which meant that he had either borrowed the shoe from a hapless *aide*, or else brought the shoe into the session in a paper bag, perhaps in the guise of a sandwich.

Whatever the truth of this, it is paradoxical that the very qualities of accessible truculence which almost endeared him to the Americans, estranged him from his own people, who applied the prim word *'nekulturny'*, or uncultured, to his excesses. It is a word applied rather differently from the way you would expect – for instance, it is *nekulturny* to enter a museum without having left your overcoat in the cloakroom – and is very much associated with tight reproving lips among the potted

Khrushchev's celebrated shoe-banging exercise at the United Nations which shocked even the Russians; a premeditated outburst since the shoe was not one he had been wearing.

plants and table-runners of bourgeois decency. The Russians clearly felt that Khrushchev had let the side down when he behaved with such abandon, and even that he might have given the impression that people all over their country expressed impulsive annoyance by banging tables with footwear.

This incident, more important than is generally imagined, together with the step forward and step back of the Cuban missile crisis, finally in 1964 excluded Khrushchev from the leadership of Soviet affairs. Compared to Stalin, he had been a lightweight, and a comic relief, except to those whose susceptibilities he had shocked. At least he was not afraid to enter the arena, to pit his potential against all comers, like a strong man in a circus sideshow. He divested Russia of a little of its mystery and, in that, his influence was most beneficial. Even if there were, as ever, secrets lurking in the wings, he made some of them almost accessible by his hot-headedness.

The colourless Malenkov had added or subtracted nothing to the sum total of Russianness, and he is easy to overlook in a swift *aperçu* of the events after the Stalin era. Brezhnev is a more substantial figure, even in appearance, with his astonishing eyebrows, raised in permanent surprise like wild windswept hedges above the cool, dispassionate pools of his eyes. It is a not unfriendly face, ready to express warmth within a general framework of misgiving.

A story is told among the thousands of others which act as safety-valves on the sensitive boiler of State, and it is typical: Stalin, Khrushchev and Brezhnev are crossing the country aboard the Trans-Siberian Railroad. Suddenly the train stops with a terminal sigh. Then all is silence. Stalin strokes his moustache for a moment of reflection. He smiles, and announces that he will deal with the problem. He alights, and comes back after twenty minutes. 'What have you done?' the others ask him. 'I have shot those responsible,' he replies.

Not unnaturally, the train shows no sign of reanimation. Khrushchev's impatience grows. He suddenly blurts out a few wild accusations against Stalin and leaves the compartment with the announcement that he will settle the matter. He returns after twenty minutes. 'What have you done?' the others ask him. 'I have rehabilitated those responsible,' he replies.

The minutes tick by, and the engine shows no sign of life. 'My turn,' says Brezhnev, without any visible intention of rising from his seat. The others stare at him for a while. 'What are you going to do?' they ask. 'I'm going to draw the blinds and pretend the train is in motion,' is Brezhnev's curt reply. There are many such pertinent pieces of irony which are created by a people imagined by some in the West to be humourless, downtrodden and incapable of fantasy.

On the face of it, anyone in Russia has a perfect right to express doubts about whether the Communist system works, since there are many indications that there is only a scant appreciation of how to achieve equitable distribution. Eggs may be unobtainable in some big cities, but within a few kilometres, elderly people are trying to sell masses of eggs on railway platforms. If fruit is suddenly fairly plentiful in a supermarket, it is unsurprising to find it due to a form of private enterprise, in which the profits go to those with the initiative to have brought the fruit to market. Hungary, with the most solvent of the socialist agricultures, has already pointed a way in this direction, as indeed was the case with the New Economic Policy, responsible for the rapid economic recovery after the Revolution.

As evidence of bureaucratic inefficiency it is possible to find groups of grandmothers mending a main road, doing a job which would more than satisfy the ambitions of the most ardent women's libbers, while a few kilometres away, in the opulent gardens of Dietskoie Selo, young men of near military age are idly spearing autumn leaves among the golden nymphs and Tritons.

It is certain that incentives (particularly for quality rather than quantity) are lacking. The right to have an enlarged photograph of yourself on public display if you do a job particularly well does not seem as effective as the more normal compensations known in the West. Russians are sceptical about rewards more suited to schoolchildren than grown people. Although medals are worn consistently by those who have earned them, there are many jokes about those who take such tokens a mite too seriously.

But it is undeniable that within a framework of inflexible earnestness, the country is changing permanently. To regard it as monolithic and petrified is to forget that all countries are subject to the laws governing human nature itself, and that whatever constraints may be put upon it these are never totally successful. Asked by a distinguished British journalist if the succession to Brezhnev was even under discussion, either at home or in the office, the high Soviet official, Mr Falin, replied, 'It is under permanent discussion, both at home and at the office.'

In other words, discussion and contention are the order of the day, as they are everywhere else, even if the face they choose to present to the world seems unnaturally placid. This is due in large to the suspicion which centuries of unpleasant surprises have engendered. They tend to mistrust the evident, and ask themselves what lies behind appearances. And behind it all is the proven conviction that vodka, the clinking of glasses, not only seals the friendships of an evening, but loosens the tongues of a night. *In vodka veritas.* Drink plays a predominant part in all northern climes, and the Soviet Union, by its own frequent admission, is no stranger to the problems it engenders. But it is not alone in this.

In Sweden, the purchase of liquor by the glass is inevitably accompanied by an aged sandwich, which the waiter solemnly advises the purchaser not to eat, since it has been sold over and over again as a statutory adjunct to the liquor. As a result, Sweden possesses the most expensive sandwiches in the world which, like wine, grow in value as they mature.

In Norway, where spirits are rationed, on the first Saturday of every month people like Hogarth caricatures may be seen talking incoherently to themselves after draining their monthly allowance. It stands to reason that for the rest of the month the tendency is towards a certain moroseness due to deprivation. The laws against drunken driving have always been particularly Draconian throughout Scandinavia, and often people going to parties in their own cars will hire students to drive them home. In Sweden it used to be the habit, when explaining the temporary absence of a friend or relative in prison for driving with an excessive alcohol content, to say that he or she was 'in China'. This was fine while

China was inaccessible, but today the information is liable to give visitors to China bad reputations locally.

Finland's drinking problem is intimately linked with that of the Soviet Union, since Finns don't normally experience difficulty in travelling to neighbouring Leningrad, where vodka is infinitely cheaper than at home. Often male choruses can be heard singing in solid if abandoned unison from under the tables of hotel diningrooms, while old Russian security guards blow whistles impotently nearby.

Visiting Russia, it is noticeable that the drunks tend to be benign and overflowing with a sense of universal brotherhood, perhaps for the very reason that they are so stiffly impassive when sober.

While dining in the Praga restaurant with Ambassador Averell Harriman, a Russian sailor entered with an expression of luminous affection on his face and an unsteady step. The seas were evidently rough under his feet. On spotting Mr Harriman, the expression broke into radiance and he threatened to fall with pleasure. Advancing, he took Mr Harriman's chin in his cupped hands and kissed him effusively, crying out 'Harriman! *Drug moi!*' (Harriman! my friend!). He was immediately seized by staff, who hustled him out to await the arrival of the inevitable militiaman, and followed by Ambassador Harriman, who did not return to the dining table for a full two courses until he had assured himself that the sailor's generous sentiments would not be interpreted as either hostile or insulting. The incident did honour to both the humanity of Harriman and the goodwill of the sailor.

Problems of alcoholism and of what is known as 'hooliganism' are the products not only of climate, but of boredom, the rigour of life which is short on escapism, or on flights of personal fancy. Certainly there are the formal escapes of ballet, of theatre, and of museums, and these are used to the full by crowds who are knowledgeable about the finer points of Victorian ballet, the infinite *coryphées* pattering about on their points in woodland glades with gestures which have lost much of their meaning and all of their urgency. There are incidents of high art in all this endless reminiscence, but the accumulation of transparent fairys' wings, romanticized kilts and tam o'shanters, to say nothing of music as cloying as Palm Court gateaux and scenery discoloured by years of carcful storage, must have a devitalizing effect on the dream world of the spectator.

There are any number of fine dancers, singers and actors, but what they perform is still carefully contrived, as though the imagination were a formal garden rather than a landscape, a roof rather than the sky.

There is no other country where soldiers, sailors, and airmen are so frequently seen in museums, not in groups, but individually or in twos. What they think as they stand in reverence before a Van Eyck or a Rembrandt is open to conjecture, and even if their smiles before a Rubens are a little more indicative of their feeling, one is hard put to it to imagine American servicemen on a large scale as voluntary visitors to Washington's National Gallery, or those of any other nations in their respective patrimonies of fine art. Still, there is a distinct feeling that whereas the desire for culture has been wonderfully stimulated in men and women who have been told from their earliest youth that art is the common legacy of an entire nation, the hunger which this has excited is not wholly satisfied by what is available. The fact that visiting theatrical companies are swamped with enthusiasm even if their standards are not particularly high, and that jazz and rock groups have the delicious effect of rain after years of drought on young people, is indicative of the readiness to accept novelty which centuries of censorship unremarkable by generosity or clairvoyance have attempted to suppress.

Russia has never been short of opinionated philistines eager to guide doubters into the confines of their own limitations. Khrushchev never tired of pontificating about painting in his boisterous manner, which proved nothing apart from his greater familiarity with ears of corn. And the consequence of the interference of unqualified arbiters into the necessary wilderness of the spirit is that the interpreter is favoured over the creator, since his job is easier, and less subject to disagreement. This, in itself, causes an unfortunate imbalance in the cultural life of a country, and whereas it leads to predictable pleasures, it is frugal in surprise.

But the allegations of the Western press about life under the tight rein are legion, and consistent. Any item of self-criticism in Russian papers, be it an examination of alcoholism, or the arrest of a profiteer selling illegal nylons, is picked up with the straight face of objectivity which unsuccessfully dissimulates a grin of glee. It is as though there were a gathering desperation to prove that the system does not work. The West makes its points as consistently as the East, but with the conviction that whereas the East is the source of propaganda, the West is a fount of honest reporting. The in-fighting within the framework of UNESCO illustrates the point very well. The accusations levelled by both sides, or at least the fears expressed, are fully justified by the divergent points of view; emerging countries wish to control their own sources of information, and this is feared by opponents of such a scheme to entail at least the possibility of constraint on free information by dictatorial, single-party governments. So far so good, but it is never acknowledged by anyone that news is, by its very nature, tendentious. An American journalist writes for an American public, a French one for a French public, and already the information is subliminally laced with the condiments to the taste of readers with habits formed by time and by tradition. This is all the more so since concepts of freedom itself vary from place to place, and have their own effect on what people in various parts of the globe are willing to accept.

We have reflected previously that the American constitution is so framed as to suggest that the government is a necessary evil, and there is

OPPOSITE: A Russian poster of 1920.
OVERLEAF: 'Reverie in a Moscow study. Little Father in his trophy room.'

8 МАРТА—ДЕНЬ
РАСКРЕПОЩЕНИЯ ЖЕНЩИН

DIE BRENNESSEL

VERLAG FRANZ EHER NACHF. GMBH. BERLIN SW 68

„Väterchen" in seinem Jagdzimmer

Träumerei an einem Moskauer Kamin

OPPOSITE ABOVE: A bride laying her bouquet at the tomb of the Unknown Soldier. This ritual symbolizes ordinary Russians' justifiable preoccupation with the security of their frontiers.
OPPOSITE BELOW: GUM department store, Moscow.
PREVIOUS PAGE: The German Army advancing into Russia.

in fact a deep suspicion of its power and its motives ingrained in the overt concept of freedom as enjoyed by Americans. Anything outside civic or national obligations is regarded as an interference in personal liberties, and to be resisted at all cost.

In Russia, all is centralized. In the human aquarium, all species are graded and live in separate tanks. An application to leave one tank for another is regarded with grave misgiving, and is invariably turned down, because a criticism of the system of grading is regarded as anti-Soviet without reference to the personal predilection of the applicant. In the United States, all the fish are in the same huge lake, and as the tadpoles go in to live their life of enviable freedom among the barracuda, the stingrays and the sharks, they are told, 'Remember, you've got rights'.

No system is perfect, yet all peoples in a troubled world feel constrained at times to defend their system as though it is. And when this defence takes the form of armaments on an ever increasing scale of bestial ingenuity and conscienceless technical advance, then we must ask ourselves if the moral issues we so devoutly invoke as the excuse for all this military megalomania are not themselves crushed out of existence by the immorality of the weapons which are intended to uphold them.

And what are these moral issues in any case? Are we fundamentally so different from each other that we can afford to evoke the elements which divide us as an excuse for an hostility graver than mere disagreement?

Freedom of thought is possible anywhere; in prison, in labour camps, in moments of solitude or reflection. No power on earth has yet managed to eradicate this right. Freedom of action is possible nowhere, unless we allow the ability of a rich person to buy an expensive object as a freedom, but this is denied a poor person, and therefore cannot be considered as a right, but merely as a privilege.

We are all subject to the rule of law, and even if the laws are different, they are far less different than we imagine. The business of living is remarkably similar in all parts of the world, except perhaps where the business of living is identical with the business of survival.

What then is the nature of the moral issues which divide this dangerous world into two camps? Ask the pious padres on American television in their tinselled jackets, and they will invoke abrasive prophecies from the Bible, alleging that the present situation had been foreseen once we accept that Communism is the embodiment of the Anti-Christ, with its greedy eye ever fixed on the sanctity of private property (which includes not only bank accounts but the human soul).

Ask politicians like Richard Nixon, less ostentatiously devout, and he will say soberly that Russia's avowed intention is the domination of the world. In this opinion he has the endorsement of no less a figure than Konrad Adenauer, but at a time when he stood at the helm of a wounded Germany, with a victorious and bristling Soviet Army on his doorstep.

Well, it may be argued, the Soviet Army is still not far off, it is still too large and too well equipped for peace of mind. Why do they need so many men under arms if it is not to unite the workers of the world in their fashion?

All arguments in this area are pure conjecture, and any one of them may be reputed by events if some fool becomes nervous to the point of mistaking a flight of migrating birds for an irrevocable flight of missiles. Nevertheless, it is worth examining other aspects of a situation too fraught with perpetual peril to be taken as lightly as do the puerile pastors of the minor airwaves.

Double standards are the order of the day. A prying camera may well manage to achieve a photograph of a Soviet prostitute adjusting her shoe after a tough evening on the sidewalk, and it may well be that she will eventually report her pillow talk to the appropriate authorities, but it is unfair to assess such a journalistic scoop without reference to 42nd Street in New York with its orgy of eyecatching come-hither neonlights, or San Francisco, where every taste is catered for with civic blessing.

Freedom is, of course, indivisible, and among its infinite facets there is the freedom to be gullible, without which the freedom of commercial acumen would find it difficult to find expression. An advertisement in a Los Angeles newspaper is a wonderful example of this exploitation of one freedom by another. 'Receive obscene phone calls from guaranteed nude girl' it reads, and goes on in its deep understanding of the human condition today, 'All major Credit Cards accepted'.

It is no doubt understood by those who find release in such diversions that this little freedom is included among all the other large ones in that composite concept on behalf of which the missiles are ranged and the bombs are primed.

CHAPTER SEVENTEEN

My Russia

The salient point of my Russia is that I am not afraid of it. In the light of its history, I do not understand how it could be other than full of profound misgivings about the intentions of other powers. This fact needs no proof apart from that which I have already written.

Napoleon's invasion was the first concentrated attempt to conquer the country with an army composed of many disparate and even luke-warm elements, which outnumbered the Russian forces at the beginning of the campaign by two to one. It was assumed, as it always had been, that Russia was too cumbersome an entity to be able to spring to its own defence with any alacrity. The alarm registered by the *Boston Gazette* of 3 December 1812 shows that today's apparently instinctive enmity did not exist at a time when neither country had been pushed into positions of predominance. 'The unprovoked attack upon Russia is nothing but a disguised attack upon ourselves. The wretches who seek to tarnish Russian prestige in the eyes of honest citizens deserve opprobrium and public condemnation for the renegades and spies they are.'

While praising the valour of Russian arms – 'they have achieved the kind of pure and irrefutable glory which brooks neither buts nor ifs', Joseph de Maistre, Sardinian ambassador to St Petersburg, nevertheless added, with pride in his origins, that, 'France is the only continental power in this universe which fights on other people's territory and never on its own.'

His proud boast did not stay true for long, but he might have added that Russia fought most of its major wars on its own territory, and but rarely on other people's. Some forty-two years later, the Russians were once again victims of Western revanchism when the Crimean War broke out without a *casus belli*. But this turned out to be a local conflict within a prescribed arena, and cannot really take its place among the invasions. However, sixty years after that, the world was engaged in a war which began almost flippantly as wars go, but soon became as uncontrollable as a plague. Russia, as we have seen, opted out of the conflict in 1917 after losing over a million casualties, and concluded peace treaties of a more or less humiliating nature with her former enemies. She was in no physical condition to continue, not only because of her losses, but because her factories were patently incapable of producing either weapons or ammunition on the enormous scale required. And in any case, with Lenin at the head of the government, she had other things to think about.

Once again underestimating Russian resilience, the Allies landed primitive expeditions with the hope of restoring a government sympathetic to their cause. Now these are facts largely forgotten in the West, for the very good reason that the armies failed in their objective, and one does not dwell too long on failures in school. But every Soviet boy and girl knows that there were British, French, Japanese and American troops on Russian soil only sixty years ago, that the Germans succeeded in occupying the Ukraine while the whole of Siberia and large tracts of land in both the north and south were virtually under foreign military occupation, and that the Soviets improvised their first major victory against all comers.

Only twenty-four years later, it all started again, this time with twenty million casualties instead of one million, and once again a victory was achieved after a muddled beginning full of costly mistakes and errors of judgment.

Is there any valid reason why the Russians should not prefer to be in a state of permanent readiness, or why they should have implicit faith in the good intentions of the West? There is far less to prove the good faith of the West than there is to argue for the sincerity of the Russians' desire for peace. The almost infinite chorus of the dead may testify to this in silence. Russia has experienced suffering in war on a scale unknown to other peoples in the last two hundred years. She has had French, British, German, Polish, Austrian, Danish, Italian, Romanian, Swiss, Turkish, Japanese and American troops on her soil as unwelcome visitors. And now she is planning the conquest of the world?

Compared to Russia, the United States has a short and blessed history. The Civil War has been their only dissent which could not be settled by argument, and it was a small thing indeed compared to the convulsions elsewhere. It has never known invasion or famine on any kind of scale. It has had a depression and a market collapse, but these are but a measure of inherent wealth, and the recovery was a proof of American resilience and optimism. Also, it emerged as a country when its problems of transport were already on the way to being solved. There was no time for local hostilities to fester in isolation. It became a coherent nation very rapidly, acquired its qualities of charming pragmatism almost overnight, and developed its extraordinary commercial and organizational talents without real opposition. This lack of threat also gave it time to develop an untrammelled idealism, which is almost more of a luxury than money. American politicians have the habit of referring to it, with a mixture of affection and awe, as 'this great country of ours', and they observe slightly archaic niceties such as placing the hand over the heart during the playing of the national anthem, which is a kind of umbilical cord linking them to the uncertainties and wisdom of their beginnings as a nation.

In the period during which isolationism was still possible, Russia was regarded as an imperial autocracy with sharp divisions of class and privilege, all that was repugnant to American sensibilities. In fact, when Maxim Gorky came to the United States to preach revolution, he was greeted with the greatest possible fervour, and it was deemed at the time that revolution was the only future for a country like Russia, that is, until it was discovered that the lady accompanying the great author was not his wedded wife, when he was asked to leave the United States. The information was leaked by the Tsarist government, of course, who knew America well enough to hazard a guess that there was nothing quite as potent as a whiff of extramarital liaison to extinguish the flames of revolutionary ardour.

Bolshevism is the antithesis of simple American faith, and we have seen that although Herbert Hoover arranged a characteristically generous famine relief for the Soviet Union in the nineteen twenties, it was not until 1933 that diplomatic missions were exchanged. In the Second World War and just after, an uneasy alliance was possible because of a common enemy, but it is striking that as sophisticated an authority as President Roosevelt should relieve himself of disarmingly ingenuous sentiments at his allies of circumstance. 'I don't know a good Russian from a bad Russian,' he said during the Teheran Conference, according to Isaac Deutscher's remarkable book about Stalin. 'I can tell a good Frenchman from a bad Frenchman, I can tell a good Italian from a bad Italian, I know a good Greek when I see one. But I don't understand the Russians.'

Here we are already more than halfway to the unadorned symmetry of Mr Reagan's vision of the world. Why, one wonders, is it necessary to distinguish between good and bad Russians? Although it is admittedly something of a relief to know that good Russians are a possibility in such a concept. And how clever of Roosevelt to tell a good Italian from a bad Italian. When a scandal like that of the Banco Ambrosiana erupts into the headlines, with suicides and evidence of squalid corruption, it becomes clear that even Italians cannot always make this distinction.

The rules of the corral, the white Stetsons versus the black Stetsons, do not apply to life, and especially not to diplomacy, where a good diplomat is one who seems to agree with you, and a bad is one who does not. And tomorrow, by circumstances beyond the control of individuals, the positioning may be reversed.

It was Roosevelt who launched the idea of four policemen whose beat was the world. The United States, Britain, the Soviet Union and China were to patrol the globe, pushing their weight around in a pleasant kind of way, and keeping it in order. Since Britain could not keep up with the others and China was in turmoil, that left the United States and the Soviet Union, and a worse idea can hardly ever have emanated from so distinguished a mind, although it did, in most respects, conform to the realities of the day. And it still does.

The confrontation has by now become so arrant, the arteries of NATO and the Warsaw Pact so hardened, that a permanent and inflexible danger threatens us all. And now that the offers of co-existence have been rejected, the brief moment of hope expressed by cooperation in space and other interchanges are things of the past, and the non-proliferation treaties are left unsigned and argued over, the temperature lowers by the minute. Already there are perceptible rifts in the fabric of the Western Alliance. American efforts to destabilize the Soviet economy by withdrawing technical assistance, even to the extent of making her allies conform to American law by applying restrictive measures to goods manufactured abroad under licence, are clumsy in the extreme, tactless, and basically unintelligent. Retrospective legislation is deeply repellent to Europeans, and it is no justification for reneging on contracts, especially those which create employment, and are of eventual benefit to all.

To think in terms of a European dependency on a Soviet natural gas pipeline is to think permanently in terms of potential conflict, and the direct consequence of this is the great scope of Soviet military preparedness. They have every reason to feel threatened by the rigidity of American policy towards her, and the increasing sharpness of tone, with petty restrictions for diplomats and other irritants like withdrawals of privileges, unimportant in themselves, but indicative of an eagerness to play a rancorous, spiteful game of tit-for-tat, as dignified as adolescent sulks.

Of course, the paradoxes of human rights on the one hand, and the adoption of a low profile on the other, have led to the superpowers conducting their affairs through surrogates in many parts of the world: Cubans in Angola and the Horn of Africa; Israelis in Central America; and of course, on Israel's own borders, and beyond.

It became clear in the Lebanese conflict that whenever General Sharon, the Israeli Minister of Defence, was accused of impulsiveness as he charged over the countryside like a bull in search of china shops, he replied that he was doing the work of the United States in eradicating traces of Soviet influence from the Middle East. Russia began to be upbraided in almost resentful terms by even her most avowed foes for not having made more than verbal gestures in the direction of her *protégés*, the Palestinian Liberation Organization. Certainly it was to a certain extent due to the extreme discretion of the Soviet government that Israel and the United States suddenly found themselves alone in the arena, and absolutely free to quarrel. The horrible massacre in the Palestinian camps brought matters to a head, and the Israeli opposition at last found a voice liberated from military expediency, and began the slow and painful process of restoring the faith of civilization in an ancient people, a people of lawmakers who seemed for a terrible moment, rather late in their history, to have found a law they had previously overlooked, that of the jungle.

In practically every one of the many local confrontations, from the Senousi to the Falklands, from the Horn of Africa to El Salvador, the superpowers do their prompting from behind the scenery, but where they are physically involved themselves, they take elaborate pains to avoid confrontation. Their weapons speak for them, but in other hands. The time for all-out folly has not yet come. At the moment, it only sells newspapers.

But if the United States acted so soundly, and correctly from her point of view, in the Cuban missile crisis, consider for a moment how the Soviet Union is placed. The Arctic, for so long impenetrable, is obviously the principal battleground for the abstract conflagration of tomorrow, if it comes. The one advantage is that there is little to destroy, apart from ecological balance, but then it will merely be a waste over which death and destruction are lobbed. Finland is a buffer zone of neutral character in time of peace, and then comes the so-called Iron Curtain, which the Russians consider necessary for their peace of mind for reasons we have examined at some length.

Endlessly to confuse Russia's military imperatives with moral issues is to sacrifice the truth to the exigencies of propaganda, that is Western propaganda. The Russians are less interested in what the Poles, Czechs or Hungarians think than they are in military cohesion of their system of defence. The unfortunate and often tragic interventions in Prague and Budapest were certainly the doing of generals and not of outraged Communist theorists. Even in Poland, where the Russians bent over backwards not to intervene physically, the danger of Polish liberalization is not so much a social one (although Russians must have been embarrassed by the resemblance between the Polish strikes and those which sparked the beginning of their own revolution in 1917). It is a threat to their lines of communication with the German Democratic Republic, and therefore a dangerous weakness in the structure of the Warsaw Pact.

To the south lies Turkey a country that is a paradoxical part of what is known as the free world, bristling with listening posts and an American military presence. Then Iran, which before the coming of the Ayatollah and his particular brand of religious fundamentalism was the most flamboyant of America's allies, a hive of modern weaponry against a background of illiteracy and backwardness. Then Afghanistan, an historical crossroad of British and Russian influence and counter-influence. Then China, who has at times offered the United States facilities for observing the Russians as part of a pragmatic anti-Soviet arrangement between powers with nothing in common.

If you translate this encirclement into American terms, you can imagine the kind of mood, somewhere between anxiety and belligerency, which would grip the United States if there were Soviet military bases along the south of Canada, most of the Mexican border, and peppering the Caribbean. Her reaction to the presence of missiles in Cuba, and her misgivings about Nicaragua, Guatemala, Honduras and El Salvador are indicative of her intense vigilance where her own security is concerned. How much more rabid would America's reactions be if she were as thoroughly encircled as is the Soviet Union? And why should there be such surprise if the Soviet Union does all in her power, under the circumstances, to ensure that she will not be caught unawares yet again, this time on a global scale, with frontiers which are hundreds of thousands of miles long? Those who consider that Soviet arms are excessive for her needs are those who also consider the honour and moral rectitude of the Western Alliance to be above reproach. There is no historical or ethical reason why the Russians should be convinced by this. From their point of view the West is doing everything in its power to exert military and economic pressure on them in order to retard their development and keep them on the defensive. In a sense they are right, at least as far as the United States is concerned. Ironically, the kind of pressure exerted, in which military expenditure is kept at an abnormally high level, with the consequent strains on Russian technical and industrial capacity, only serves to hold back liberalization and an improvement in the standards of living. The less pressure there is, the more Russia will be able to advance along the road she has been following for centuries, defeat her old enemy, distance, once and for all, and enter more fully and cooperatively into the comity of nations.

European countries tend to understand this, hence certain accommodations to which America objects so strenuously. After all, Europe has lived with the giant during its infancy, its childhood, and its adolescence, and although a certain inherited fear may still exist, Europe suffers as an entity from its sharp division into two camps – East and West, into two economic systems, and worst of all, falls between two ruinously expensive and essentially sterile dispensers of death.

There is no permanent future in deterrence, just as there was no permanent future in fears of hell fire as a way to enforce morality. To attempt to take the curse off the potential horror by speaking of a limited nuclear war is about as sensible as asking a man to consciously limit his intelligence. It cannot be done.

Let me say it again, I do not fear my Russia. It is a land with a poignant history of survival, a past incredibly rich in contrast and the unexpected. To make claims for it is neither my mandate nor my inclination. I do not believe in the superiority of peoples, and I believe even less in their inferiority. The Russians are intrinsically people like any other, who have qualities and defects, and the world would be a poorer place without them.

If there is anything to fear from them, it is not at all because they have over four million men under arms in peacetime, simply because 'peacetime' has not been peacetime for half a century now. It is rather because to them life is hard, and they feel instinctively that this has to be so. It is something to grapple with and to come to terms with. Its joys and pains are to be savoured to the full, and when there is little to eat, little will be eaten. This endless proximity of catastrophe has given human relationships a special direction. Friendship is emotional, tears are not an embarrassment but a spontaneous token of involvement, physical contact is not eschewed. Men can be seen kissing, or walking with their little fingers entwined.

It is consequently a race capable of great spontaneous communal effort, with a capacity for personal effacement for the common good. It has demonstrated this ability time and again, and it finds expression in a fervent love and appreciation of nature and things natural. It is also unusually open to poetry. A poet reciting in a public place can cause a traffic jam. And, of course, Russians are inordinately sensitive to the rhythms and harmonies of their own music. This appreciation of life as hard, and its secrets as accessible to the open-hearted, gives them a fibre common to all Slavic peoples. On the other hand, the United States is endowed with an advanced sense of civic responsibility of a quite different sort. These are qualities of separate peoples, and yet they make them complementary in the vast spectrum of human possibility.

If, however, you were to invite the American people to live as the Russians live, the offer would be immediately and effusively rejected. They would be horrified by the monotony, the drabness of life, and its lack of creature comforts. Believe it or not, the American way of life would be as curtly rejected by most Russians. The smell of roses hardly compensates for the absence of thorns. The proof? The Russians voluntarily abandoned Hawaii, whereas the Americans made it their 51st State, and increased the voltage of the electric guitars.

The Russians are deeply attached to their miseries as well as to their joys. Their literature and music have made an artistic pleasure of sadness. The well of melancholy is bottomless, and laughter is a close relative of tears. Russian exiles suffer more from the absence of this pungent perfume of sorrow than other exiles seem to miss whatever they have left behind, and they try to recreate it wherever they go. In order to understand the Russians, it is worth knowing that no other people speaks so shamelessly of the *soul*, not for want of a better word, but because it is a correct description of that aching void which is not a void at all, but a nerve sensitive to everything.

If they seem stiff and unsmiling in their official guise, is this not an act of voluntary discipline to eradicate an erratic and searching spirit? It is the only country I know in which a policeman will write out a ticket for a dirty car. What is this if not one of many efforts to eliminate an age-old tendency towards sloth and idleness instilled by the frigid winters and immensity of the country?

Its enemies think of it as a huge prison camp. In fact, there is a problem of overcrowded prisons everywhere. And yet, the prisons in themselves are not the problem, but rather the reason people find themselves in them. My Russia is not a prison, but more a school, sometimes even a kindergarten. It is a place that seeks to impose discipline as schools do, and both the discipline and the rules continue into adult life. Khrushchev broke the rules, and was expelled. Others suffered worse fates in the bad old days, but today there are perceptible and welcome changes. These may not be solutions to those who regard concensus in the Western sense as a necessary adjunct to freedom, but Russia has no alternative and no need to solve her problems in other ways than her own.

The fact is that, contrary to the opinions subjected to the influence of prejudice, it is as possible to make good friends in the Soviet Union as anywhere else, and to keep them, to argue with them, and even on occasion, to see eye to eye with them. The Russians are, as I have said, a people like any other, even if they are subjected to the imperatives of a great social experiment which is clearly not to every taste.

'What about the KGB?' I can hear the outraged shout. 'What about Afghanistan?'

It is not my intention to whitewash or to condemn, but merely to strike a balance which I believe essential if we are not to head willingly and with reprehensible docility into a future of increasing danger. I will therefore refrain from even whispering back, 'What about the toleration of "dirty tricks" and the activities of renegades of the CIA? What about Viet-Nam and the Dominican Republic?'

To join these choruses would be merely to lose the voice of moderation in the fashionable babel of accusation and counter-accusation. Superpowers have codes of behaviour germane to them, which the rest of the world find at times difficult to understand. The United States entered the Viet-Nam war for reasons which seemed logical and necessary to the military. The war went on for years, and the high moral tone became degraded by events. Nobody cancelled any Olympic Games because it was admitted that even if the war was an aberration, America's heart was in the right place, and she was big enough to learn by her mistakes.

Long afterwards, the Russians entered Afghanistan, for reasons which seemed specious to all but her most fervent allies. This time the Olympic Games were disrupted, and the tone became shriller all round. Mark you, it could well be that Russia was anxious about her Muslim minority, nineteen per cent of her population and increasing faster than the Slavic element, as the wave of religious fundamentalism spread elsewhere like a forest fire, obeying no borders, and appealing to allegiances much more ancient than Soviet power. But nobody looked for reasons in this case. Naked aggression was sufficient, and in need of punishment.

Both wars were unnecessary and hideous. To the defenceless people in an Afghan valley or a Viet-Namese forest, or even in Beirut, the origin of the bombs which rained on them were of as little concern as the moral rectitude of the men releasing them. Gratuitous death is a crime whatever the moral posture of its perpetrators.

It is a regrettable fact of life that the CIA and the KGB seem to be necessary, and those of us from smaller nations, can have no influence on such phenomena. When France and Britain tried to behave like superpowers at Suez in 1956 it was a total failure, strangled at birth by the USA and the USSR in curious unison. Since then Britain has had to be content with James Bond or 007, who is far more fun and far more lucrative than dull reality.

I do not think for a moment that I can influence minds which have been made up. I can only tell my story to those with the generosity and, dare I say it, intelligence, to preserve an open mind. To them, and to them alone, I would say in ending that my Russia is a land which has found expression in many different ways, all deserving of, at least, our attention.

Russia's early survival was a miracle: her youth a torment; her adolescence merely dangerous; her maturity a series of challenges. If now she has been called to a shared pre-eminence, her recognition of the folly and horror of war is a measure of her responsibility, not a mask for her desire to conquer the world.

In the final analysis, he who wishes to conquer the world, deserves it. And he is a fool.

If I am unable to influence those who have refused to follow me thus far, I abandon my right to a last word for their benefit to no less an authority than Joseph Stalin. He remarked to the American politician, Harry Hopkins, 'Even if the Russians are a simple people, the West often makes the mistake of regarding them as fools.'

Illustration Acknowledgments

The museums, libraries and photographers who supplied the illustrations are kindly thanked for their cooperation and are listed below. If in any case the acknowledgment proves to be inadequate the publishers apologize. In no case is such inadequacy intentional, and if any owner of copyright who has remained untraced will communicate with the publishers, a reasonable fee will be paid, and the required acknowledgment made in future editions of the book.

COLOUR PLATES
Bridgeman Art Library, 86, 153 *(above)*, 187 *(above)*
Countess Bobrinskoy Collection, 51, 85
Gamma/Frank Spooner, 208 *(above and below)*
Hamlyn Group Picture Library, 120, 188
Robert Harding Picture Library (Photos Victor Kennett), 52 *(below)*, 187 *(below)*

Michael Holford, 52 *(above)*, 119 *(below)*
MacClancy Collection, 119 *(above)*, 154, 205, 206, 207
Nationalmuseet, Copenhagen, 18
Rainbird (Robert Harding Picture Library), 17, 153 *(below left and right)*

MONOCHROME ILLUSTRATIONS
Bildarchiv Foto Marburg, 71
Countess Bobrinskoy Collection, 46, 72, 83, 111
Boudot-Lamotte, 23
Lord Brabourne, 132, 133, 134
Bridgeman Art Library, 55, 101
British Museum, London, 54 *(below)*, 67
CLI/Keystone, 179, 180, 197
Deutsche Fotothek, Dresden, 78, 124, 128, 130
Hamlyn Group Picture Library, 20, 21, 27, 28, 31, 39, 67, 73, 79, 89, 115, 117, 126, 145, 159, 199
Robert Harding Picture Library (Photos Victor Kennett), 37, 75, 96, 99, 113, 114, 127

Michael Holford, 33, 54 *(below)*, 92
Kansallismuseo, Helsinki, 147
Kungl. Biblioteket, Stockholm, 43, 49, 62
MacClancy Collection, 9, 10, 11, 12, 135, 156, 160, 166, 169, 172, 190, 191, 193, 194
John McGreevy Productions, 2
Mansell Collection, 95
John Massey-Stewart, 32, 40
New Century Pictures, 141, 144, 148, 149, 151, 158, 161, 162, 165, 171, 174, 175, 182, 184, 192
Novosti Press Agency, 24, 34, 35, 42, 65, 107, 116, 150, 177
Popperfoto, 104, 105, 125, 136, 137, 138, 139 *(above)*, 139 *(below)*, 200
Rainbird (Robert Harding Picture Library), endpapers, 6, 54 *(above)*, 58, 60, 64, 69, 112
Svenska Porträttarkivet, National Museum, Stockholm, 76, 80
Roger Viollet, 56, 61, 66, 88, 102, 108, 123, 129, 131, 140, 143, 173
Victoria & Albert Museum, London, 33

Index

(Figures in *italics* refer to captions to black-and-white illustrations, and those in **bold** to colour illustrations)